The
Investment
ZOO

Transcontinental Books
1100 René-Lévesque Boulevard West
24th floor
Montreal (Quebec) H3B 4X9
Tel.: (514) 340-3587
Toll-free 1-866-800-2500

Library and Archives Canada Cataloguing in Publication
Jarislowsky, Stephen A.
The Investment Zoo: Taming the Bulls and the Bears
Includes bibliographical references.
ISBN 2-89472-259-1

1. Saving and investment. 2. Investment analysis. 3. Speculation. I. Toomey, Craig. II. Title. III. Series.

HG4521.J37 2005   332.6   C2005-940536-8

Copyediting: Trish O'Reilly
Proofreading: Elaine Rogers
Author photo: Laurence Labat
Page design and graphic concept: Studio Andrée Robillard

Printed in Canada
© Transcontinental Books, 2005
Legal deposit — 2nd quarter 2005
National Library of Quebec
National Library of Canada

ISBN 2-89472-259-1

We acknowledge the financial support of our publishing activity by the Government of Canada through the BPDIP program of the Department of Canadian Heritage, as well as by the Government of Québec through the SODEC program Aide à la promotion.

Stephen A. Jarislowsky

with **Craig Toomey**

The Investment ZOO

Transcontinental Books

Contents

Foreword

Investors today are surrounded by predators, much like in a jungle. Governments are possibly the biggest predators of all. But stockbrokers, advisors, underwriters, executives, bankers, and organized labour, not to mention lawyers and accountants, all take a slice out of investors' assets. *Caveat emptor* (let the buyer beware) is always good advice.

Much of our savings in Canada literally goes to waste. Keeping money in cash or bonds accomplishes little in the long term after tax and inflation. Generally speaking, real estate, over long periods, cannot do much more than track inflation and the rise in per capita national income. Otherwise, over time, few people would be able to afford lodging. Stocks representing company equity have a life little different from that of human beings: Unless they are sold at a profit or earn significant dividends, the journey from birth to death leads from near nothing to near nothing.

Two other great enemies of successful investing are your own greed and fear: When markets are high, investors become increasingly greedy; when stocks or markets are low, fearful. High market prices need not necessarily be a danger to the long-term investor, but they are for the short-term one. Low prices, on the other hand, can be buying opportunities — or just another pitfall if the company goes "bust."

Calm nerves, a good game plan, and some basic knowledge are essential. Hunches can play a role but should be checked out thoroughly before being acted on.

This book is based on some 50 years of investment experience. The idea was brought to me by my friend Harry Schaefer of Calgary, who travelled to Montreal to tell me there is a need for this book, especially today, when there are so many small investors being corralled by slick mutual fund salespeople and other marketers. I agreed with him and felt compelled to put some observations about the "investment jungle" on paper.

Chapter 1

A Life Fully Invested

Anyone reading this book — my first at the age of 79 — may want to know who I am and why they should bother paying attention to my opinions. The story is long, much like my life, but I'll try to be as brief as possible:

I come from a family with a long history of industrial and private banking activity dating back to my grandfather, who owned a steel mill in the eastern part of Germany. He also had interests in coal and banking and was extremely successful for a time. He had a horror of waste, a trait that I share. There was no question of throwing out a piece of paper that had been used on one side; he would save it and write on the other side. A simple shack served as his head office — which his general manager remonstrated with him about. "Why change?" my grandfather responded. "It has served us just fine up till now." He personally supervised many of his company's activities and would often arrive at the gate of the steel mill at six in the morning to see that his employees got there on time. He was involved "hands-on" in all aspects of the business and retained absolute control over all expenditures. This is a family trait. I have it and my father used to have it. I think my children also carry it in their genes.

I was born in Berlin in 1925, one year after my brother Axel. My father died from scarlet fever when I was four years old. He was only 30 but had already accomplished a tremendous amount since taking over the family business from my grandfather in 1923. In fact, he had been hailed as a financial genius, and whatever newspaper clippings I have read attest to his exceptional, albeit brief, career. Unfortunately, the financial-industrial complex built by my family fell to the Nazis in the 1930s and was nationalized by the Communists without compensation in 1947. We are still negotiating with the German government to get some of those assets back, or at least to get compensation.

My mother, who trained as a lawyer and was a very strong-willed woman, gave birth to my sister shortly after my father's death. Because she had to look after the affairs of my father's estate, in 1930 she decided to send my brother, sister and me to Blaricum, a small town about 20 miles from Amsterdam in the Netherlands. She rented a house for us there and equipped it with help — a chauffeur, a cook and a maid. It wasn't far from my uncle and aunt's house, so they could keep an eye on us.

My aunt and uncle to a large extent became our surrogate parents. My uncle managed a company that had been importing goods from Asia since the seventeenth century. He was a very fair and ethical man who was somewhat of a socialist and I admired him greatly for his generosity of spirit to his employees and family. During World War II, he provided shelter to dissidents of all kinds, be they Jews or Communists.

My mother came and visited us in the Netherlands from time to time but was mainly preoccupied with business affairs back in Germany. I attended elementary school and was an eager student, ranking first in my class. I also studied music and frequented the museum in Amsterdam, which had a large collection of works of art by the great Dutch masters. I also began to collect art books. Art became a lifelong passion.

In 1934, my mother remarried, and three years later, she and my stepfather decided to move the family to Paris. In those days, an upper class education on the Continent meant acquiring fluency in French and English. So I was sent to the École du Moncel, a secondary boarding school run by Swiss Calvinists near Paris, for two years. Then the Nazis invaded France and we made a quick retreat to Aix-en-Provence in the south. My family settled into a hotel there, while my sister and I were sent to local boarding schools. In time, I moved in with the art critic John Rewald and his wife and immersed myself in books about the Impressionists, further cultivating my interest in art.

While I was still a very good student, I didn't really enjoy school all that much. I had found it difficult being suddenly uprooted from my life in the Netherlands and transplanted to the École du Moncel, where I knew no one, in a country where I didn't even speak the language. But I forced myself to adapt quickly and learn French. At the school in Aix-en-Provence, during the winter of 1940–41, there wasn't enough to eat. Sometimes one side of the table would get the food, another time, the other side. It was a typical Jesuit school: You got a good education, you slept with your hands above your blanket at night, and so on. But I viewed all these experiences as challenges to be overcome — failure has never been part of my vocabulary.

My stepfather had worked with the French bureaucracy, and in Marseilles he became very active in getting people out of France to the US — scientists and all kinds of people who were in danger. He worked with Varian Fry, a Quaker-educated American who helped save thousands of endangered refugees who were caught in the Vichy French zone. Some of the people he helped wrote back to their relatives and friends to say how they had gotten out of France. The Gestapo intercepted several of these letters and it became clear we'd have to get out of France rather quickly.

We boarded a transatlantic ship called, oddly enough, the *SS Winnipeg* and left France in March 1941. We stopped in Algeria and Morocco, then crossed the Atlantic with 1000 French sailors who were being sent to reinforce the garrison of Martinique, where France's gold was being stored. From there, since my stepfather had an assignment from the French government to go to New York, we went to the US by way of Guadeloupe and Puerto Rico. We arrived in New York in April 1941.

Fortunately, we had money in New York, as my father had invested some $100 000 in 1924 — a fortune at the time — in the US, guided by a friend, the president of the investment banking firm Dillon, Reid. While my mother was busy looking after these investments and the rest of the family, I was sent to preparatory school in Asheville, North Carolina for tenth grade. After skipping the eleventh grade, I graduated in 1942 with a good grounding in the classics and proficiency in several languages: French, English, German, and Dutch.

I then enrolled, at age 16, in mechanical engineering at Cornell University in Ithaca, New York. The US had already entered the war, but I received a short deferment from military service on reaching 18 years of age. Having lived through the fall of France, I knew what war looked like. I remember being in Paris one day in May 1940, lying in our garden, when maybe 400 German bombers came over and dropped their loads on the Paris suburbs. I also saw German planes firing on the people who were fleeing Paris on the roads. And later, on our way to New York, I witnessed the destruction of the French fleet at Mers El Kebir in Algeria.

But after graduating from Cornell in 1944 at nearly 19 years of age, the US Army decided I should now join up. Uncle Sam Wants You! While only a landed immigrant at the time, I became a US citizen very rapidly when I was in basic training at Camp Blanding, Florida. The army couldn't send me overseas unless I was a US citizen, so they herded us foreigners into a truck, drove us into Jacksonville, and asked us to swear allegiance to the United States. Since I had already been in an ROTC-type program in France, I knew more about the military than the average guy who got drafted and I quickly adapted. I was acting squad leader in boot camp during basic training.

After completing infantry basic training, I was exposed for the first time to East Asian and specifically Japanese and Chinese studies. This included written and spoken Japanese under the Army Specialized Training Program at the University of Chicago, followed by a brief sojourn at Camp Stoneman in the San Francisco Bay area. After this, I spent a year with the US occupation forces in Tokyo. When I first arrived overseas, in the Philippines, they asked for somebody who could type 80 words per minute. I volunteered even though I typed with two fingers. They soon decided I would be better suited for work as a special investigator for the US Counter Intelligence Corps in Japan.

I enjoyed this period very much and was intrigued by the culture, which was totally different from those I had been fortunate enough to absorb in earlier years. My interest in Japanese culture continued to grow during my time there, since I was able to observe and spend considerable time with Japanese people, and got along very well with them. Knowing the language was a great help, of course. I had done an enormous amount of travel for someone my age and had been exposed to a large number of languages and cultural values. I have always been very adaptable to different cultures and traditions. In other words, I could act as a German, a Frenchman, a Dutchman, or an American. And because of my work in intelligence, I was exempt from normal occupation duty and was able to dedicate my time to meeting and interviewing people in positions of authority, a valuable opportunity that I made the most of.

I had been a very eager student in university and my inquisitiveness continued on the ground in Japan. The fact that many of the students I had met in Chicago were Japanese Nisei (second generation) immigrants helped the transition, as did the many Japanese people I met in Japan. I was involved in the "de-Nazification" of German nationals, many of whom were people doing research in Japanese studies, which again helped me further to understand Japanese customs.

One of my tasks in counterintelligence was to interview Germans and determine which ones were Nazis and should be deported. I didn't know it at the time, but the investigative techniques I learned then would prove very useful in my subsequent securities research. It was in Japan also that I had my first experience with "governance." My unit learned of a rumour that the wife of General Douglas MacArthur was trying to influence the choice of contractors in the post-war reconstruction. When unit members began asking questions, Washington temporarily suspended our operations.

On my return to the US in the fall of 1946, I was eligible to study under the *GI Bill of Rights*, which provided financial support for returning veterans. So rather than look for a job as an engineer, I decided to take a year off to pursue my studies of the Far East, which I felt were incomplete. My stay in Japan had merely served to pique my interest in the region and its cultures. I returned to the University of Chicago for a one-year graduate degree in Far Eastern history and culture. That was a master stroke, since I had as professors three of the world's leading authorities in their fields: Chinese History, Far Eastern Art, and Comparative Far Eastern Religions.

These courses were essentially seminar courses and the university believed in graduate students working at their own speed. It was an incredible opportunity to explore more deeply the cultural values and ways of thinking of the Far East. I wrote a thesis on the cultural revolution in Japan in the sixth, seventh and eighth centuries, the period of the Tang Chinese cultural invasion of Japan. This helped me put into perspective what went on in Japan under the US occupation right after World War II, another period of cultural transformation and upheaval.

During my studies in Chicago, I wrote several essays that were to influence my approach to life and my investment philosophy for years to come. In one of these essays, titled "On Understanding," I arrived at a very simple and obvious conclusion: True understanding of something can only be achieved by oneself. In other words, to understand something, you first gather information, then think it through, synthesize it, and decide what it means and where it leads. Nobody else can do this for you!

Descartes said it simply: "Je pense donc je suis." This precludes blind belief and blind acceptance — you have to think something through fully yourself to understand its meaning and the consequences. In my essay, I then added that this inevitably means a call to action based on one's own understanding, as life must be lived and not left fallow.

For me, the essay "On Understanding" was a major turning point and revealed to me the process I would have to follow to live my life with self-respect. But what would be my call to action based on the understanding of my life experience to date? My life so far had resembled a chess game always played defensively: Being pushed from country to country and from school to school. Having no true family life with my siblings and parents. Two-and-a-half years studying engineering, which meant extra credits each term and courses all year round. And, finally, the army and its regimented way of life. Having everything forced on me rather than being able to decide for myself required me to adapt quickly and be self-reliant. Otherwise, I wouldn't have survived.

But now I had finally reached a point in my life where I could take matters into my own hands. My Oriental studies, as well as those in comparative religion, made me decide that I would devote my life to being "an example to others." From Japanese culture, I had learned about the importance of "precedent" — of setting an example — and, from Western culture, the importance of leadership. My idea was to marry these two great concepts from different cultures in the way I would conduct my own life. This thought, along with the idea of understanding being the result of personal reflection, has been a major motivator for me ever since then (though not the only one by any means). Rather than bemoan the constant upheavals of my youth, I began to see them as precious experience that I could draw upon.

My genes also told me that it was time to earn some money — and to believe myself capable of doing it. My initial idea was to make a million dollars by the age of 40 and become a US ambassador to Asian countries, preferably to Japan. That was my ambition. But unless you were willing to spend years working your way up in the bureaucracy, you had to be rich to have a diplomatic career. At least that's the way I saw it. I also wanted to be independent financially. Money doesn't mean reckless spending, but it does mean freedom. You could quit your job, do something else — do exactly what you want, without worrying about what other people say or think or want you to do.

To me, money has always been a means to an end, not an end in itself. While I was a student, I always lived on a very small allowance. When I married my first wife at the age of 22 in 1948, we lived on the $105 a month provided by the *GI Bill of Rights*. I never touched a penny of the capital I inherited from my father. I lived off my income and continued to do so when I started working.

Even today, I don't know how to spend money. It's a habit I have never been able to get rid of. I have lived in the same house in Westmount, Quebec, with my wife, Gail, for the past 32 years. I've never been drawn to material goods, except for works of art. Big houses, boats, private planes — they don't mean a thing to me.

After living through the war and the Depression, though, I knew that money was important. Yet apart from what my family and people I knew had told me, I didn't have a clue how to make it. I had never really earned money.

Up to the age of 22 I was either studying or in the army — and even there I was taking courses. I felt that it was time to come down from my ivory tower and enter the real world.

I had figured out that I didn't want to be an engineer or a teacher, even though the University of Chicago had offered me a post when I graduated with my MA. Instead, I applied to the Harvard Business School, where I was accepted to start in September 1947. It was logical that I would go into business, but I decided that I first needed to study it to "understand" it from the bottom up.

Harvard Business School was really more of a trade school than a university, after the wonderful intellectual feast at Chicago. We were required to pore over various case studies from morning till night — 50 pages of this one, 100 pages of that one —which led to nothing in the end. Then we'd have to discuss them with 100 students in the class, which led to nothing either. There were few texts that treated these issues systematically and in depth. This was frustrating for someone who considered himself an "intellectual."

Nevertheless, Harvard took my fears of business away. I learned about manufacturing, which fitted in with my engineering training. I had always been good at mathematics, so accounting and finance came quite readily. I had never done any sales or promotion, but that didn't appear overly difficult. Human relations and administration had much in common with getting along in boarding school and the army. In the second year I discovered investments, and more particularly corporate finance and banking. Because of my family history, it didn't take me long to feel comfortable in these areas.

I graduated from Harvard with an MBA (distinction in Finance) in 1949; seven of my classmates would go on to lead Fortune 500 companies. I wasn't sure what to do next though. Success has always been very important for me, but I also felt a strong need to find something that would give me a sense of belonging. I felt like an outsider with no "network." When you're young, it is hard to know what path to follow —Is this the right one or will I just end up wasting a year of my time? It's like walking around in the dark — you start to make things out, but you're still not sure if you're getting anywhere.

I was married by now and this clarified matters somewhat since I now had no choice but to "get going" and make some money to support my wife and myself. Fortunately, a Harvard Business School degree at that time was a desirable commodity for large US corporations, which had to renew their executive ranks following the Depression and the war, and members of our class had many job offers. Before accepting an offer from Aluminium Limited (now Alcan Inc.), I checked out the company carefully through the university library and financial reports. It passed my in-depth review and the job seemed promising, allowing me to combine engineering and finance with the prospect of international travel and even a foreign posting.

I started in August 1949, first as a sheet mill engineer in Kingston, Ontario for about three months, then briefly in international sales at the Montreal head office. The first time I visited my future hometown the only thing I knew about it was that it was in Canada. I stayed the first night at the Windsor Hotel and the next day when I went out I was surprised to notice that people were speaking a language I already knew — except the accent was difficult to understand.

Shortly after transferring to head office in Montreal, I was appointed assistant to Dana Bartholomew, the director of finance of the holding company. A graduate of Yale and Harvard, Dana was a bit of a loner in the company but was a friend of the Davis family that headed Alcan at the time. He had a strong intellect, was highly individualistic, and was to become my good friend and mentor.

Working under Dana, I was put in charge of capital appropriations screening, based on financial criteria as well as working capital and cash forecasting. Later, I went into the supervision of Asian and African subsidiaries for the holding company. While not aware of it at the time, this was an excellent introduction to security analysis and good investment practices from the inside of a large corporation. It taught me how one worldwide corporation went about its business from a vantage point near the top of the pyramid. I also was editor of Alcan International's in-house magazine that kept executives around the world informed of the corporation's results and objectives.

While a seemingly successful young executive at the age of 25, I became restless and didn't see a rapid career ahead. My boss had at least 25 years to go and I didn't relish being appointed chief financial officer of a subsidiary somewhere. I had been working constantly, always giving more than required. I noticed that I had a capacity to work 10 times harder and 10 times more quickly than people around me. That meant that, 90% of the time, I was drawn into political intrigues within the company. After a while I found this tiresome, and it irritated me that I had to send out so many copies of everything on which I needed a decision. Eventually I got very frustrated by the process because I like getting things done. I don't like sitting on my hands and waiting for the politics.

So when my in-laws died in New York, I asked for a leave of absence from Alcan to run the family business, an art book publishing company. It was here that I further nurtured my passion for art and art collecting. My personal contact with painters and critics allowed me to deepen my knowledge of painting. But it didn't take long before I found the city claustrophobic. And as the father of a young child, I didn't see it as a good place to raise a family. I also couldn't see myself running a publishing company for the rest of my life. So in time I sold it to a large competitor, the New York Graphics Society, and became, for a short time, relatively unemployed. We had bought a house in the Town of Mount Royal shortly before the death of my in-laws, and so we returned to Montreal, where I had some ideas for developing a business or two of my own to feed my family.

I decided not to go back to Alcan and instead, to keep myself amused, started a number of different enterprises with friends as a kind of hobby. These ranged from a laundry in Laval owned by acquaintances of my wife's relatives to an aluminum impact extrusions company established with the son of Alcan's president, as well as mutual funds in petroleum and mining. I also started a financial statistical publication based on the techniques of analysis I had used at Alcan. That's the kind of doodling I was doing at the time: dabbling — trying to get people started in different operations.

One of our ventures was mining. We represented a company in New York during the building of the Campbell Chibougamau mine in Quebec. I remember driving my car up there; the roads weren't very good for the shock absorbers. The general impact extrusions business was quite successful. I was the first president, then somebody else more professional took over, and it was sold much later to Consumers Glass. The laundry, which offered a door-to-door service, didn't do as well — in fact, it went bankrupt.

This experimental period of my business life went on until 1954, when I teamed up with my friend, Jack Brown, who had worked in public relations at Alcan, to develop a statistical service delivering data on various companies. The idea was to provide brokers and investment dealers with a tool to help them with their research. In about a year, we developed reports on roughly 200 Canadian companies, including simple balance sheets, income statements, interim results, and certain ratios covering a five-year period. These statistics allowed you to see whether profit was rising, whether capital investments were paying off, and how solid the company was in general. They gave a pretty good view of the quality of management and how a company compared with others in its sector. This work started as a hobby, but led to a business that is now nearly 50 years old.

After six months of this last venture I had a disagreement with Jack and bought him out in December 1955. Since our original investment was only $100, it didn't cost me very much. I then hired a secretary, Stella Scanlan, and an assistant, Rolf Halle, a Norwegian fellow. After a squash game with Scott Fraser, a friend of mine who worked at McLeod, Young, Weir and was a bit of a free spirit, I asked whether he'd like to join this venture.

And so Jarislowsky Fraser was born. We found that there wasn't enough business for our statistical review — we had sold 200 subscriptions and that pretty much flooded the market — so we had to do something else if we wanted to make money. My background lent itself to doing field research: meeting company executives and writing up studies on what I found. I began to do custom research and eventually we were retained by an investment counselling firm out of Chicago. This also led to our being put on a monthly retainer by big houses in New York and London, England.

Eventually, because of our research and the fact that people recognized our skill, several corporations gave us a mandate to help manage their pension funds. Some of our earliest clients were Celanese Canada, Steinberg's, and Canada Steamship Lines. We also worked with such companies as Sun Life and Royal Trust when owners felt they were not getting the right attention. From that base, we branched out into investment counsel for individuals, endowment funds, and other pools of capital.

It took us the best part of 10 years to earn a decent income for ourselves. It's a very slow process if you start from nothing. After all, why would anyone hire you? People would ask us, "Who are your clients?" and we'd reply, "If you hire us, we'll be able to say you are our client." We often wondered whether we were going to make it.

We never looked far ahead though. We still don't. I just do what I think is right and keep moving in that direction. I don't believe in five-year and 10-year plans. I've planned my life a great deal in many ways, but not in business.

If something comes up and it interests me, I'll go in that direction. Many people drift into their line of work and I was no exception. But I also believe that you should choose an occupation that comes naturally and in which, because you have the right personal attributes, you can excel. Work that frustrates you or sends you home dissatisfied causes stress and, if continued, may warp your outlook on life and hurt your self-esteem. In that case, it's better to change and endure some temporary insecurity in order to find your true gifts and inclinations.

In our company, at times I spotted people who I knew were not made for our line of work. In the worst cases, we fired them, explaining that, while it seemed harsh in the short term, in the long term it would be in their best interests — allowing them to go on to discover their true skills and thrive. In other cases, such as when a security analyst really would never reach the top of that profession, we transferred him or her to sales and client service. I remember two associates who benefited greatly as a result. Their knowledge of research was a major advantage in their new vocation and allowed them to shine.

While unplanned, Jarislowsky Fraser has turned out to be my main life's work. Apart from a prolonged drought in the early 1990s, when we lost over a third of our pension fund business, the firm has had steady and uninterrupted growth. We are currently one of the largest private fund management companies in Canada, managing investment funds on behalf of governments, corporations, universities, other institutions, and labour unions, with assets in excess of $50 billion.

This growth has been based on a constant philosophy that has changed little over the years. It is a philosophy based on serious field visit security research and investment in excellent, growing companies. We have tried to work diligently to make our many clients steady money at low risk and at a fee that has always been in the low quartile of our industry. As such, I believe we have set an example to the industry.

Over nearly half a century our business has followed a path that was built one stone on the next. We were never in a hurry. We did our job as well as possible, did not diversify, except geographically, and stuck to a basic, rational philosophy that has been refined and implemented by the best people we could find. We trained our people from the beginning and rarely hired those with long years of experience elsewhere. This has led to an individualized culture in our company and a relatively low staff turnover.

Our firm's philosophy is founded on conservative, time-proven principles of fundamental investing. We construct diversified, high quality portfolios that are designed to protect existing capital and achieve long-term growth for our clients. This investment approach has produced consistent, mostly above average investment returns through changing economic environments. It has been particularly effective in minimizing the volatility prevalent in today's global markets. Fundamental to our success is investment in proven, well managed, high quality companies that are financially sound — and this investment is always supported by intensive field research. Each year, our investment professionals follow more than 200 Canadian, 150 American, and 150 international companies, including frequent visits to many of these companies.

Our mission has never been only about business. It has also been an attempt to do what is right and ethical. We have consistently advocated good governance in Canadian public corporations and have fought many corporate battles to make sure our clients receive fair value in takeovers. We have pushed for corporate governance that is investor friendly, not self-serving. The clients who entrust their funds to us must receive good results over time and must, even in the worst times, like the years 1999–2003, feel that they are in good hands, despite the inevitable losses in times of a major market crash. They must also know that we are truly professional and will defend the integrity of their capital to the best of our abilities. This is in a period when integrity in business has been seriously compromised, both in the operations and ethics of the companies in which we invest, as well as in the investment industry generally.

As chief research analyst at Jarislowsky Fraser for nearly four decades, I have analysed practically every industry you could think of, and have been involved in a lot of them. I believe that I know how to judge a business situation and how to appraise management. I don't just use statistics to come to conclusions; I do a thorough analysis of all aspects of a company's business.

I also believe that I know how to run a company and could be CEO of a major corporation. I have been lead director of many companies and still am for one or two. If you want to be a good investor, you have to know how a company operates and how good the people in the company are. And you have to understand the industry and how it works and who the other players are. In many ways, a company is like a painting: you have to be able to take it in. There's no sense in seeing it other than how it should be seen. You have to focus on it to really know it.

Having sat on about 20 boards of directors, I feel that I also know what directors do, what the chairman does, how to deal with executives, and how to ask them questions. They know who I am and they're not going to tell me lies or nonsense. For them it's a two-way street. If I were appointed to a board like Alcan's today, I would be able to go in there and, after just a few sessions, be very effective. I know the issues they'll discuss. I know the industry, how it functions and what kind of management it has.

Being active in other corporations as a director has allowed me to continuously build my understanding of the internal workings of the type of companies in which we invest. It has taught me to clearly appreciate what makes a great company and has allowed me to experience the pleasure of participating in something that succeeds beyond expectations. It has also brought me into contact with innumerable very fine people, many of whom I have come to count as wonderful friends over the years.

I like solving problems, getting things done, and seeing the results. Going into a company as a director and cleaning it out is a lot of fun. I participated in such a process in British Columbia in 2003. The culture of this company had to be changed. So we appointed a different president and watched the changes percolate through the entire organization. I have always believed it is important that the companies in which we invest have top-notch management and executives.

I have certainly made investment mistakes. Everybody makes mistakes and you don't learn unless you make a few. There are always surprises that nobody can foresee. On a short-term basis I am quite impatient and easy to anger, though like a storm cloud, it passes over rapidly and dissipates; I'm not one to carry long-term grudges or smouldering anger. I don't mind other people making mistakes as long as they're not stupid mistakes — and as long as they don't make them twice.

When a company we were involved in turned out to be poorly managed, we did not just sell — though there have been times when we had no choice. But in many instances, especially in a takeover situation, we have stood up and fought to protect the values of our clients and to get better terms. There have, however, been instances — unfortunately too many — where the laws and the deep pockets favoured the corporations rather than the investor. And in most cases the securities commissions were nowhere to be seen.

Moreover, securities laws and regulations are highly influenced by the corporate sector and, in turn, by well-paid lawyers. They too often see the minority investor as a nuisance once they have his or her funds in hand. Rarely do securities commissions act based on fairness and ethics. Unless something is clearly proven to be illegal, a call to the regulator is a pointless gesture. In the cases where the commissions have acted, its lawyers, comparatively ill-paid, have been no match for the high-paid lawyers of the predators. Moreover, some cases have dragged out for years: Justice postponed indefinitely is justice denied.

Our focus on championing good business practices fits in with my philosophy of trying to help people. I've found that having done things for others has brought an enormous amount to me in return. I really believe that if you have a certain code of ethics, you should live by it. I guess that's just a personality quirk. I don't know where it comes from. It could be insecurity, attention seeking — a desire to be loved and honoured. Who knows?

In fact, a number of human insecurities have probably led me to this kind of mindset and this type of work. But I've always believed one should live up to one's responsibilities and do the best one can. One of my biggest influences was the nineteenth century philosopher Søren Kierkegaard, who espoused a very individualistic, anti-dogmatic view of religion and stressed the importance of individual actions and accomplishments. My philosophy is that in business you're like a bond: you pay 5% interest, you have a sinking fund, and at the end of 20 years you pay the principal. You do everything you are supposed to do to the letter, and that's it. Private life is more like an equity — it's less predictable. If you want to get yourself into trouble in your private life, well, that's your decision. But the moment you come to the office, please leave it behind.

At Jarislowsky Fraser, we've never wanted to make money just for the sake of it. We have the lowest fees in the industry. We could easily add millions of dollars to our revenue without losing business. But that's not our function. Our function is to look after people's money and make sure that they make money. If we make money in the process, fine! But the first beneficiary has to be the client.

Unfortunately, ripping off clients is very common in our industry today. I'm not talking just about investment counselling but to a large extent about underwriting firms and mutual fund companies. It's pretty evident what they're all about: Charge the highest fees possible and make as much money for themselves, not the client. I think that if there were more professionalism instead of greed in our industry today, everybody would be better served.

Since the investment zoo is full of unpleasant and greedy people, my goal has been to bring them to light whenever I can. I have often written letters to regulatory authorities when I felt a company was abusing its shareholders. Sometimes I have even been able to get this kind of behaviour exposed in the newspapers. My hope is that this publicity will temporarily do some good — and in the long run may even change securities regulations. It could affect people who otherwise wouldn't have been touched. But I'm also a realist. I'm under no illusions that I'm going to change the world. My approach has been to just say what you have to say. If people object to it, that's fine. If they listen to it, that's fine too. If you don't expect very much, you'll always be pleasantly surprised. I'm fully aware that during your lifetime, you may be able to have a small influence. But you won't change the human animal.

The most dangerous people, in my view, are the great idealists. The Hitlers, the Trotskys, the Maos, the founders of religion. They're trying to change human nature. The only problem is human beings aren't and never will be perfect. Even if you have a communist state, that doesn't mean the guys at the top of the pinnacle aren't going to rob the state and their colleagues blind.

I was guilty of idealistic thinking in my youth. I thought that the moment an idea was discovered, the whole world would immediately understand it and put it into effect — and the world would turn into a Garden of Eden overnight. The whole system of teaching liberal arts at Chicago was based on this idea of Great Ideas, "the history of mankind." But has it changed human nature? No. It may have modified it, but not fundamentally changed it.

I see myself as someone who tries to do something in a decent way and has no envy of others. I don't try to get money out of other people's pockets by hook or by crook — or by overcharging. I don't believe in the hereafter; my education by Calvinists, Jesuits, and Episcopalians left me basically an agnostic. I can't see myself sitting silently and quietly on top of a cloud for the next million years. That would be awfully dull. Those ideas are the inventions of humans. But that doesn't mean that ethics and behaving responsibly don't have a place in the universe. To me, the ethics of Aristotle *is* religion.

I am still working today because I believe I can still make a contribution. I don't believe retiring to Florida would be intellectually stimulating. I can't see myself chasing a small ball from morning to night and being terribly happy when I score something under my handicap. I don't think that's a life's ambition or that we're put on this earth to do that. That's just filling time for which you have no more meaningful use.

I've always been curious to know how different people think and act and what motivates them and where their logic comes from. I've been extremely hands-on. I believe that it's important that people know that you are running a business closely and keeping abreast of all the areas of the work. The only area I don't know is the computer. I've never been interested in learning it! I know what it does and how to make judgments as to what you want with respect to a computer's operations. I know what you look for, what questions to ask, and what not to do. But to operate it myself — the Internet would just get me fascinated with too many things and be a terrible distraction!

Because of my inquisitive nature, I've always had hobbies. But they change. They may go from wine collecting to Chinese art, music, or antique furniture. I'm interested in all kinds of things, mainly cultural. My appreciation for art goes way back to my time in Europe. I've always been interested, and started actively collecting art when I was in Japan. Collecting is just like buying stocks: You want to buy the stock at what you judge to be the right time and you want it to be in an absolutely superb company. What's the difference?

I've also gotten tremendous satisfaction from being involved in different charities over the years. We have the Jarislowsky Foundation, of course. It was set up many years ago and our company contributes money every year. So far, we've accumulated capital of about $50 million. Our main function has been financing university chairs. We have 12 right now. I am also involved in helping to set up a prostate cancer information centre for the province of Quebec. When you get to my age, you don't have any financial ambitions. I don't even take a salary from the company. Money becomes a responsibility more than anything else.

The job of guiding Jarislowsky Fraser for these past nearly 50 years has been a career that has provided me with great satisfaction and an immense variety of experience. The firm is now in the hands of a second generation and, apart from myself, only one of the early partners is still active. When I reached 65 years old, the *Globe and Mail* carried a headline: "Jarislowsky retires." Quite correct. But then, what is retirement? Is it not to spend time doing what you always wanted to do? Well I'm still doing it. My work has always been a hobby — and it remains so today.

Chapter 2

The Hijacking
of a Terrorist Calamity

Successful investment requires a sober and realistic assessment of the social, economic and political environment in which we live. My classical education and early life experience had a profound impact on my world view — one that has remained virtually unchanged for 50 years. I abhor extremism and movements based on blind ideology, religion, or "isms." I am skeptical about the competence of our governments and have found few politicians worthy of admiration. I am not fooled easily by false promises and rosy predictions. I have no use for anything that isn't in the middle of the road and puts misguided emotion ahead of common sense and rationality. I believe in moderation and individual rights and take the long view in almost everything I do.

So if I were to take a snapshot of the world just a few years into the new millennium, what would I see? Basically, an economy and a political system that are not functioning well, despite what the politicians would have us believe.

The United States is almost the only really strong, productive nation. In Canada, productivity is lagging, and consumption is rising faster than wage gains, leading to high debt levels and a stock market that often trails that of the

US. In Europe, unemployment remains extremely high, and productivity also lags behind levels in the US. In most countries, taxation is too high and social laws are a disincentive to investment. Africa need not be mentioned: Overall, it is marked by ethnic strife, dictatorship, and embezzlement. In Russia, chaos reigns. South America is making little progress, as old habits and culture prove serious obstacles to economic stability, and larceny has not diminished. With a few exceptions, it is hard to justify serious investment there.

In the Far East, Japan is swimming in government debt, which would have been crushing had interest rates been at world levels and not at 1% per year. Cultural constraints there dampen individual ingenuity, while living standards are too high in relation to the rest of Asia to be competitive, especially compared to China, Taiwan, and Korea. Southeast Asia remains muddled in selfish politics, dubious ethical standards, and worse.

On top of this, political events have severely shaken the world. Human nature being what it is, fanaticism has always existed. Large collective organizations — whether nations, tribes, or religious groups — have always been at the heart of war, mass hatred, and prejudice. Countries that base their systems of government on individual rights rather than dictatorships have been far less exposed to these organized hatreds. But with increasing globalization, individuals all over the world, even in countries whose systems of government are designed to discourage organized hate, are caught up in these unproductive causes. As a result, people tend to resemble rabbits in a meadow: The arrival or even the fear of a wolf or fox leads them to panic. And fear has certainly gripped the world in the aftermath of the 9/11 terrorist attack on the US.

However, I don't believe in being deterred by doom-and-gloom scenarios. The threat of terrorism is 80 or 90% trumped up, and its impact on the economy is exaggerated. The world's economy was in recession before 9/11 — the result in part of consumers' finding themselves overextended after a decade of prosperity and a zero savings rate. With the disappearance of the "wealth effect" — which had been based on high stock markets and the high-tech "dot com" bubbles — exacerbated by reduced earnings and rising unemployment, the time had come to expiate the sins of gluttony and overindulgence. The consumer had to save again, repay debts, and get over the hangover caused by a 10-year binge.

Recession is normal after the type of stock boom we witnessed in 1929 and in the late 1990s. But its effects this time have been mitigated by unusually low interest rates and by the US Federal Reserve pumping huge amounts of money into the American banking system to be loaned out for consumer spending. When the low interest rates didn't work, taxes were cut to a level that has now caused the US to have a massive budget deficit. And when that wasn't enough, the US administration decided to devalue the American dollar to make the US more competitive and to export the recession to countries like Canada and Europe. US manufacturing jobs, meanwhile, continue to be exported to cheap labour markets like China.

Because of these artificial measures, we really haven't felt the crunch yet. As long as the present situation persists, we cannot expect housing and consumer spending, based on low interest and debt, to go on indefinitely. If the US dollar continues to fall, as it has since 2003, the people who own bonds and cash outside of the US may increasingly want to liquidate them. And in order to counteract that, in time, the US will have to increase interest rates quite materially. This will create a very difficult environment for the consumer. On the other hand, with the 2% short-term rate, it's not exactly enticing for foreigners to buy American government bonds. Basically, we've been trying to prevent a recession, and the only way out of the mess eventually is through inflation to get rid of all these debts.

These economic realities are being overshadowed, to a large degree, by what has frequently been touted as a "terrorist calamity." Yet I believe there is no such thing. This "calamity" was initially hijacked by President George W.

Bush for political reasons. There is, and always has been, terrorist activity in every country where people in government steal right, left, and centre. You would expect that many people would object to this behaviour on the part of their leaders. 9/11 was an attempt by certain Islamic groups to tell the US that it's not totally invulnerable and that its actions taken in the Middle East are unfair. I don't consider local resistance fighters who are doing the killing in Iraq to be terrorists any more than the French, Czechs, Hungarians, and Poles were terrorists when they fought against the Nazis occupying their countries during World War II.

Obviously there was terrorism, but not on a scale that necessitated a "War on Terrorism." In fact, I believe that Mr. Bush has contributed to the rise of terrorism in Afghanistan and in Iraq. People in those countries basically don't agree with the United States occupying them, don't like colonialism, and don't like to be represented by a bunch of phony politicians. Americans are naive if they think they are going to bring democracy to these countries, which have not had democracy in 10 000 years. They have little understanding of cultural values in these countries. You couldn't change American culture in a week, so why should you be able to change a culture that is thousands of years old in two weeks?

The Middle East is clearly a major flashpoint for political unrest in the world today, and I believe that sooner or later the situation there does have to be dealt with. Essentially, religious states like Israel or Iran should become something of the past. They really are not *religious* states. They are simply home to people who identify themselves as Jews or Shiites, whether they are observant or not. I don't believe that there is a need for religious states of any kind in today's day and age. Why not be a tolerant country like Canada? The English people in Canada didn't say, "Nobody can come in here unless the English faction is over 50%." Having second class citizens is, in the long run, simply not workable. South Africa tried it — and failed.

The State of Israel, which also has two classes of citizen, has produced nothing but instability over the past 60 years. Clearly, there's a critical need for a peaceful compromise, a way for both peoples to live together. Creating hatred, *à la* Sharon, is not the way to establish a permanent peace. Sooner or later, the area has to be defined, and I believe that the frontiers have to be guaranteed internationally. A lot of my Jewish friends agree with this, while others feel I am an anti-Semite. I tell them that by being even-handed towards the Palestinians and the Israelis, I cannot be anti-Semitic, because they are both Semitic peoples. But they don't look at it that way. That doesn't particularly bother me, because I think that in the long run what I'm saying is rational and logical.

To march into a country without any justifiable cause, like the Americans did in Iraq, to overthrow the guy who's in charge, was unjustified. Why not march into about 50 countries in the world tomorrow morning? Why pick on only one?

I believe that Mr. Bush's "War on Terrorism" — and his view that anybody could be a terrorist — resembles what the Nazis said about the Jews. Hitler said that it was the Jews who were behind every terrible thing that ever happened to the German people. By fanning patriotism in the US and using the excuse that "we are at war," Mr. Bush has been able to stifle criticism. This is very far from a real democracy that sets an example for the rest of the world.

What Mr. Bush's policies have spawned is in many ways McCarthyism on a major scale. And there is no doubt that most thinking and educated people in the US who have travelled can see right through this. Mr. Bush has not done the Americans any good by making them come off as even "uglier" than they were before. He is basically destroying what America stands for. For my money he has flouted all the things we fought for in World War II — democratic values, the rights of the individual, the "free society." I find it absolutely ridiculous that someone my age has to take off his shoes, turn his belt buckle around, and open his zipper when trying to catch a plane at the airport.

I have been an admirer of the US system in the past, but I think that what's going on right now boils down to "think our way or you're not patriotic." I'm sorry to see that many people in the US seem to take the attitude "we are a semi-master race" and "we are better than everybody else." That again, is the kind of thinking that I saw in my youth and have never appreciated.

I'm proud that Canada did not follow in America's footsteps with regard to Iraq. I believe we don't have to do what the Americans say and that we should maintain a much broader perspective and a more humane point of view. We don't have to go along with actions that are motivated only by a desire to be re-elected and not by principles of international justice.

However, this does not compensate for the fact that the Canadian government has been mismanaged for a number of years. Fortunately, ours is a very rich country, so to a large extent we can afford this mismanagement. But our standard of living is definitely lower than that of the Americans on average, and there's no real need for that.

One of our problems is that we have no real opposition at the federal government level in Canada, except in rare times of a minority government. The June 2004 federal election, which resulted in a Liberal minority, represented an improvement, I believe, since it served to keep the politicians on their toes. But history shows that minority governments don't prevail in Canada. This points again to the need to update our democratic institutions, including instituting an elected Senate. The fact is, for now, the only real opposition in Canada is posed by the provincial governments. They have far more power than individual states in the US. Indeed, we are almost a federation of provinces rather than one country.

The dominance of the federal Liberal party is the legacy of Brian Mulroney — and is also due to the fact that nobody cares. The average person in Canada is largely apathetic towards government. Apathy and low expectations are major problems in this country. We are not a crusading nation, nor are we idealistic. Canadians are mainly concerned with their own well-being. As long as each individual is reasonably happy, that's all that seems to matter.

As a result, excellence is very difficult to attain in Canada. It is not something that people by and large aspire to. They want to have a pleasant and easy life. We don't have any external enemies to stir us out of this indifference. The only enemy we used to have was the weather, and we've conquered that pretty well with modern heating systems and automobiles. When there is a cold spell here you can get from your home to the office without exposing yourself to the elements. You simply go from one garage to the next. You don't even have to leave home if you don't want, because you can communicate by computer, e-mail, or telephone — except that your better half might not want you there; he or she didn't marry you for lunch!

A Chinese immigrant to the West who returned to China is reputed to have said that Canada is a first-rate country with second-rate people because they elect third-rate governments. I share that view and I have even come to believe that most governments are a country's or province's worst enemy. It is not that I am an anarchist, as clearly we need law, its enforcement, and many common services — water, roads, etc. Winston Churchill said that democracy was "the worst form of government except for all the others that have been tried" — in other words, the best of a bad lot of governments. I agree with that also.

The reality is that in peacetime, or when things are not plain awful, democracies tend to produce very poor government. This is not confined to Canada. It seems universal. Only when things are very, very bad — in times of depression or war, for instance — do we have sound people come forward to put common sense and efficiency back in front. The reason is quite simple: Politicians intentionally confuse being elected with giving good government. "After all, if the people didn't want us, the other guys would be in," is their credo. How do you get elected? By taking the money of those who have earned and saved and giving it to those that have not. Since there are always more of the latter, it is an easy formula for getting a majority.

In Canada, low productivity, a dismal savings rate, high taxes, low investment, and high unemployment, as well as the brain drain, can all be laid at the door of an antiquated form of government, run by people living to be re-elected. This government has placed self-perpetuation through massive vote buying policies ahead of long-term economic progress. As is now becoming quite evident, this is a self-defeating strategy in the long run.

Despite its shortcomings, the US form of government still stands above that of Canada and many other countries in the world. I'll explain why. In Canada and in much of Europe (with exceptions such as the Netherlands and Switzerland), we have centralized power, an enormously costly social safety net, strong labour unions, and an emphasis more on collective, rather than individual, well-being. In contrast, the US government in times of peace is so choked by checks and balances that there is little internal concentrated power. Neither the Executive Office nor the Congress have that status. The emphasis is on the individual and his or her happiness and development, not on the collective. This has meant relatively lower taxes, strong incentives for each individual to do well, weak labour unions, and less emphasis on helping those who cannot help themselves. The result: greater labour mobility and adaptation to economic realities, more individual fear and greed. In other words, self-motivation!

I also admire the American drive for excellence and their belief in charitable giving. I tend to be a little more patriotic toward the Americans as a result of having served in the American army and receiving my entire university education in the US. This, in a sense, causes me to still identify with them. When you fight in a country's army, either for right or wrong, you identify yourself with it. However, I don't identify with the born-again religious right in the US. I also very much deplore that Americans won't face up to the fact that bad times are a necessity. You simply cannot maintain good times indefinitely. That doesn't mean that there should be extremely bad times, but I don't agree with a lot of the selfishness and excesses that we have seen in the stock market down there.

I believe cultural norms will need to change in most areas of the world for them to become truly economically competitive. Forms of government must also be adjusted to emphasize individual rights. This demands the creation of checks and balances to restrict government power. With this must go an improvement in the brain quality of those who make government decisions. This is a huge task. It may require many quiet revolutions all over the world. But not attending to it in time may lead to not-so-quiet upheavals and seriously impede economic progress.

Chapter 3

The Perils of Debt and Over-Consumption

The world's real problem and the greatest threat today is not terrorism but excessive consumption and debt. The problem of social costs being geared to good times, never mind average — and certainly not poor — times is also significant.

Politicians all over the world have practised the "art of the possible," not the art of the mean balancing both extremes. When an extreme became possible, they grabbed on to it to buy the most possible votes. In the emerging economies of the world (Indonesia, Russia, Thailand, and Argentina, for instance) the idea was to become industrialized overnight, with all the necessary infrastructure. That required money and borrowing proved easier than saving, politically and emotionally. Unfortunately, debts have to be repaid. But when the creditors asked for the money back, the money had already been spent. These nations now reap the consequences.

This over-indulgence has been fuelled by television and the Internet, which have been telling all on earth what constitutes the good life. And people around the world have been "going for it." Rising stock markets and rising real estate prices made it seem safe to spend and adopt a higher standard of living. Those who couldn't afford it any longer cashed in capital or borrowed, since giving up the good life is neither personally pleasant nor politically popular. And so we arrive at the present world impasse. Only the US and some European countries — those that have lived with capitalism for a long time, such as England, the Netherlands, and Switzerland — have retained some sense of reality, although not a very conservative one.

Overspending led to overcapacity, especially in raw materials, which many emerging countries developed with huge foreign loans. No wonder resource prices spiralled downwards in the early 2000s and led to deflation, not inflation. As the poor, populous countries built factories, they undersold those countries with high wages and strong labour unions. This too led to a deflationary trend. Moreover, as some of these countries now face insolvency, their currencies collapse causing them to produce yet more cheaply, thereby exacerbating the world problem.

Deflation causes more debt, because lower prices increase the weight of debts as things get cheaper, converse to inflation. Countries such as Argentina and Indonesia that experienced a currency collapse also saw a good part of their domestic currency debt wiped out — but not the foreign pay loans. In those countries, all those who could fled to dollars or Deutschmarks or other currencies that might hold value. In Argentina in particular, the weight of foreign debts became a crushing burden.

As loans collapse, the world banking system weakens. Bad loans reduce bank equity. Because the world's banking system is increasingly unified today, any problem is a global problem. As nations collapse and their purchasing power crumbles, the sales and earnings of international companies are also affected.

I believe that debt worldwide is so high that a sharp expansion of the money supply, which in time always causes inflation, is inevitable. With deflation, lower living standards lead to less tax collection and, unless nations are willing to resort to a major abandonment of social services, it takes years to emerge from the mess. While low inflation may still be with us for a while, I doubt that governments will be re-elected on a deflationary platform, as it will mean our gradual impoverishment from excessive debt. As standards of living and stock market wealth drop, luxury items will have to take a back seat. Only the rich will be able to afford them. Capital expenditures will fall and so will the earnings of those companies that cater to this sector. Raw materials prices will fail to make a comeback as world demand drops. The high-tech sector will still do relatively well, as remaining current in this area has become a "must" for companies that want to remain efficient and competitive and lower their costs. Mergers will continue, as efficiency based on computers favours large companies in many industries.

The excessive taxation we see today also frustrates the saver of income. It reduces the savings rate and, the consequence is even lower employment rates. Taxing the investment return of those who normally reinvest the money continues to kill jobs and hurt the economy.

Taxation has never been fair, since government can only take from those who have money. One of the major results of excessive taxation is that it materially retards jobs and development, both of which require investment. There is an ages-old puzzle about which came first — the chicken or the egg. Well, between investment and jobs, we know that investment comes first.

It is time that business and investors strongly opposed a system that levies such high taxes on investment income; this fiscal burden slows down job creation, thus contributing to unemployment and leading to a horrendous waste of people's skills. Unless the population understands this, politicians will continue to buy votes at the expense of job creation. I accuse politicians of having killed both jobs and the economy and I accuse the population of letting it happen.

High tax levels discourage both work and investment. Our brightest and wealthiest people are leaving. There are three million Canadians in California alone! Compared with Canada, taxes there are low; the weather and the way of life are great. In the current economic climate, Canada is in effect using Canadian tax dollars to educate our young people only to see them become US taxpayers for life. Still, our politicians insist that to get the 18-year-old vote, we must provide university education for a few thousand dollars per year, something that costs the taxpayers many times that amount. The best students are then hired away by US corporations at double the salary they would earn here. We have a shortage of good young doctors in this country. Why? Because here they work for far less, get taxed to death, and are over-worked in poor, crowded facilities. Why wouldn't they leave?

In parts of Canada personal income tax is at a record high and on average the taxes on family income exceed the cost of food, shelter, and clothing combined. Capital gains taxes over long inflationary periods are clearly confiscatory of capital. So why stay — why invest? The savings of the average Canadian, formerly around 10% of income, are now nil.

If we had savings and these were wisely invested, we would have more jobs, less tax, and more investment. And this would have a multiplying effect as it does in the United States. A dollar given to the government is simply spent and remains only a dollar; a dollar invested in productive jobs generates more dollars, which, in turn, can be reinvested, generating more dollars — and so on.

Assume your company earns a 20% rate of return and this amounts to $100 000. If not taxed, you would keep $100 000. Assume now that you can reinvest to also earn 20%. In five years your $100 000 grows to $248 832. If the government, however, takes 50% in taxes on your investment income, you are left with $50 000, which, because of tax, you can only reinvest at 10% after tax. The $50 000 in five years becomes $80 525. Question: Which sum creates more jobs and more wealth for the country?

With higher inflation on the way, for the reasons stated above, the economic situation in Canada is certain to get worse before it gets better. Consumers, who have been keeping the economy going with high levels of spending for several years, are particularly vulnerable, especially if they come to the point where they feel they can no longer keep up the pace. Older people who are dependent on fixed incomes are also very vulnerable if interest rates rise and bonds fall. I am already seeing a lot of people, older people, cashing in capital in order to maintain their standard of living.

This is not a healthy development. Overall, a lot of people are trying to shelter themselves by moving away from monetary assets. Gold, art, and antiques have all taken off in price enormously. People are saying, "Well, these are real things." We know that eventually, with our excess debt, the value of monetary assets is going to decline, and even if it doesn't decline, the current inflation and taxation rates provide zero real return on bonds and cash bank accounts.

At the present, people are also moving from money into stocks, for the simple reason that the stocks will survive whatever happens, whereas it is almost impossible for the value of money to survive in the long term, given our level of debt and monetary expansion.

I too have greater faith in real values than I have in monetary values, especially at a time when governments are printing money at an enormous rate. This level of spending cannot be continued indefinitely. Nobody's going to buy a car every year. Nobody's going to buy a house every year. Nobody's going to rebuild a house and refurnish over and over. You get little from the bank for your money today, so it is obvious you should try to invest it in something that will give a real return.

Historically, real assets have always outperformed monetary assets in the long term. When I was a young fellow I could buy a Coke for five cents, while now it would cost me $2. If I had kept in bonds all the money I spent on those

Cokes, the result wouldn't buy me very much today — for each five cents invested, probably not even a single can of Coke! So cash is good as a holding action but it does not offer long-term protection. If the stock market collapses and you have money to buy on time, then it makes sense to hold cash. Other than that, nobody's ever gotten rich owning cash.

I have paintings for which I paid $300 but which are probably worth $100 000 today. If I'd put that money into bonds, it still would be worth around $300. I paid $20 000 for my first home, a semi-detached with four bedrooms in the Town of Mount Royal in Montreal. I don't know what it's worth today but probably a lot more than $20 000 — in fact, it's probably worth $400 000 to $600 000. So I don't think that keeping your money in cash is an answer.

So what do you invest it in? How do you protect yourself? I have always believed that a diversified stock portfolio is the answer, composed largely of companies in industries that are growing relatively rapidly. If you can buy those at a reasonable price, I think they are very worthwhile investments in the long term.

I think the main idea in investment is to not do stupid things, and the same is true in business. You don't want to make the wrong move in a company and have to live with it for the next five years — while you sort out a problem you could have avoided in the first place.

In the investment business you always have to look at the downside because that's where your risk is. Anybody can live with the upside! So ask yourself, "Where can we make a mistake? Where is the danger? Have we covered it? Are we reasonably protected?" We can't be 100% protected, but putting less emphasis on one stock and having a lower weighting in many others will allow us to feel more secure; we mitigate the individual risk. That's what you have to do.

You have to be optimistic as long as you're alive. You're going to be dead for millions of years! There are going to be changes, dangers, and all kinds of uncertainties. Changing interest rates, threats to a country's security, the politicians stealing too much, a change in the direction of politics, terrorism, trade wars … all these things can happen. You cannot foresee any of it, because if you could, you'd never do anything! You'd be totally paralyzed. So buy the best managed companies in the best managed industries where you know the company is big enough that one guy can't really steal the whole thing. Get out quickly if you see accounting that isn't regular or they pump up the balance sheet. But all things being equal, stocks, over any 25-year period for the last century, have outperformed bonds. And that makes sense, because why would anybody at all go into business if you could make more money on a government bond?

Therefore, in good times or in bad, I recommend you stick to the highway of investing in well-performing stocks. You'll end up the better for it regardless of the world situation.

Chapter 4

Corporate Crooks

We've seen outrageous conduct on the part of corporate executives in recent years. Along with many brokers, investment dealers, consultants, accountants, and lawyers, they share one trait — greed! This has encouraged major excess, including mismanagement, dishonesty, and outright theft. Many companies have been uselessly destroyed by such greed; even some of the largest have been badly damaged by mismanagement, largely based on short-term gain strategies. Many of the problems we've witnessed in the corporate arena have been linked to salaries, bonuses, options, and pensions for executives that in many instances have been deep in fantasy land.

It is not too difficult to understand how this greed develops. Assume there is a CEO, age 59, some four to five years from normal retirement. To date he hasn't saved much because he always tried to keep up with other "top dogs." He now has just three years in which to feather his nest, and the board gives him 500 000 options per year. If the stock goes up, he can make $500 000 for each point increase — on just one year's option!

Temptation? Is he Christ standing on the mountain with the devil? After all, his pals on the board voted this option. It is perfectly legal! The big shareholders pester him regularly about the price not rising fast enough. Need one say more? Is the long-term good of the company served? Maybe the directors have options too and are close to 70, the year retirement is mandatory. The Lord's Prayer says, "And lead us not into temptation, but deliver us from evil." Human nature is subject to temptation. If not, the prayer would not need to sound a warning.

Option plans, whose net value exceeds $1 billion in some cases, strike me as obscene. A difference in pay between a CEO and the next officer of as much as five to 10 times surely does not promote teamwork. For such a totally overpaid CEO to then turn around and put hundreds of people on the street is callous.

That boards of directors go along with such legal theft from the shareholders, for whom they are the fiduciaries, staggers my imagination. As a director on many company boards over my career, I have fought such excess tooth and nail, and there are many of my colleagues on boards who will testify to that. As a firm, we have always insisted that options not exceed 5% of outstanding shares and that they be fairly distributed among the rainmakers in the company and don't go only to the CEO. To be honest, I prefer no options at all — to anybody!

So who have been the real winners in stocks in recent times? The guys who didn't need to gamble, took no risk, and made a fortune. And if things went sour, they just had their pals deal them in again. I'm talking of the executives of the corporations, who with their annual options, their annual bonuses, and inflated salaries made zillions. Who dealt them in on the compensation committees of the boards? Typically other CEOs or board members who didn't want to lose $40 000 to $60 000 of easy money director's fees — or their association with the "Lords of the Universe." But all this money comes out of the shareholders' pockets.

How do they do it? Well, they set a budget that is not too tough and then meet it 100%. Result: They get a 100% bonus on their already inflated salaries. If they only reach 90%, they may even get a lesser 50% bonus. If they are in the oil business, when the oil price goes up, they can even get a bonus on the gain from the higher price. Some guys are also dealt in on pensions and might get a cool $1 million a year for life. No wonder they can retire early. Good thing, because what incentive would they have left to stay and work their butts off?

If you say to somebody, "Commit a crime for me for $10 000," he'll look you straight in the face and say, "Who the hell do you think I am?" It's an insult. But if you couch it the right terms and then indicate that there may be $1 million at the end of that rainbow, he may say, "Well, I don't like what you're saying, but I'll sleep on it and let you know in the morning."

The moment people start grabbing for compensation far beyond the value of their services, there is no real value to their services anymore; but greed can demand any value, any price. And that is precisely what's happened in these corporations. These people saw tennis players, football players, hockey players, and basketball players get enormous sums of money that they also don't deserve, and they featured themselves as "stars" of the business world. They hired all kinds of consultants who were happy to oblige because they got nice fees. And when the other executives heard about it, they hired the same consultant rather than someone who would advise them to keep a lid on things. So greed begat greed begat greed, until the thing exploded.

But greed will always be there, and it is necessary to come to terms with that side of human character. In effect, you have to ensure that you do not allow it to go beyond a certain threshold of responsibility and decency. If you do, then you're beyond responsibility and decency. And then anything goes. If your competitor gets $20 million and you have the same job, you can always find somebody who will point out to your board of directors that your job is bigger than his. But this goes totally against the whole idea of how to run a company well. Because how can you have teamwork when one guy gets $20 million a year and the other people get $300 000? And imagine the cut-throat competition that is created within the company between the various people who hope to succeed this guy who gets the millions? In other words, the whole process, when it's taken to extremes, becomes totally wrong. Again, much of the blame can be laid on options, which were originally designed to help retain talent in a company. Instead, they have become de facto bonuses and have encouraged fraudulence.

Options are one of the most disgusting aspects of the corporate greed we are seeing today. Jozef Straus of JDS Uniphase in 2000 got an option for 9.6 million shares. The stock was then selling at about $100 per share. The value above the strike price of all his options at year-end was $1.13 billion. Assume he exercised this option and the company wanted to buy enough shares back to have the same number as before exercise so as not to have dilution. The company would have to put out some $1.5 billion pre-tax, as the cost would be after-tax money! Obscene? At least Mr. Straus is an entrepreneur and built the company. But don't tell me he isn't devoured by sheer greed. He already had great wealth. Would you truly want this type of guy to look after your interest in the company? Not me. I would never touch stock in a company where I knew this was going on. Sure it is legal! All you need is to name the right people to the board. But are directors not supposed to protect all shareholders?

This same game is going on in many companies where the top executives are not entrepreneurs. Maybe not on the same extravagantly obscene level, but obscene nevertheless. The bank presidents of earlier times, if they were alive today, would turn green with envy if they saw what current bank presidents are getting in salaries, bonuses, options, and pensions. Was the earlier group really that much worse at their jobs — or were they simply damn fools not to have gotten the idea themselves? What risk do these people take? Almost none. The options cost nothing. Where were the directors who voted to award them? My guess is in the CEO's pocket — at any rate, they were certainly not thinking deeply! Investors should do something about this rape of the companies. They can, on their annual proxies, vote against all options that exceed 5% of the shares outstanding and against *all* options if the CEO and other top people arrogate too much for themselves.

It is time we woke up. As investors it is our money. And don't tell me these people won't work for less. As a matter of fact they might work harder, as lean cats move faster than fat ones. They might even concentrate more on the company and less on their own greed! I prefer a sincerely dedicated person to one dedicated solely to his own rapaciousness. And don't tell me you're paying these amounts to ensure that you get good people in management. These well-fed CEOs are the self-same executives who are putting out the many "earnings warnings" these days — the same people who are, in fact, doing a lousy job of managing. What example is this for those who work for them? How can such an executive then say that costs must come down and 5000 people must be let go? Isn't it time that investors, and especially institutional ones, call a halt to this racket? Aren't the investors the owners?

If we can condemn the greedy and unethical practices that go into making a bad executive, what, then, makes a good executive? Honesty and integrity are important, of course. Also a good brain and having one's feet firmly on the ground. Knowing that one has to have an excellent, well-controlled organization. Not just sitting back and playing the top man or woman, but mingling with people. Getting to know all your employees, inspiring them, and getting the best out of them. Openness and transparency are also critical. I personally don't believe in hiding things from the people I work with, ever. I don't believe in holding things back: If someone does something I don't like, I tell them I don't like it. If they do something good, then I give them a pat on the back — although I may ask in the next sentence, "What are you going to do next?"

There is no place for vanity in this business, and executives who think they're better than anyone else are making a mistake. You can't rest on your laurels. It doesn't matter who you are, you have to be on your toes all the time.

Good managers must also show initiative and take responsibility — not only for their own work but for those they work with and who look to them for leadership. They must not be prima donnas, scheming to further their own careers, but people who are looked up to and can be trusted for their leadership, loyalty, and humanity. These latter traits speak of experience, self-confidence, and a strong awareness of others, including co-managers and employees on the inside and shareholders, customers, and the community on the outside. The shareholders are the owners and their claim is foremost, but not exclusive. Their claim is best served if all inside *and* outside responsibilities are being heeded, setting aside both sentimentality and meanness. There are times to say "no" and times when "yes" must be the word.

Essentially, good management looks to the long-term as the real horizon. Short term decisions will always be made in the context of overall long-term objectives. To accomplish this, there needs to be a strong company culture that sees things in terms of long-term goals. Such an outlook is achieved very gradually and requires a careful balancing of the emotions of greed and fear — and avoids following "Pied Pipers" who promise fast gains. It demands solid and consistent performance, eschewing extreme risks, but remaining open to opportunities.

Good management leaves very little to chance. But neither does it mean over-conservatism . It requires constant renewal, but renewal that keeps its feet on the ground. It is based on sound leadership and on teamwork that accepts and feels secure in that leadership. It can tolerate strong egos but only of those that can bend for the common good. It is a framework based on mutual respect, even perhaps a degree of affection.

Good leadership of this kind builds a strong, ever-renewing culture. Criticism and ideas are encouraged but are not accepted or implemented unless they are constructive and cogent. Competence is a must and the culture insists on it. Occasional mistakes are regarded as inevitable, but unnecessary mistakes are not. They are an absolute "no-no!" Discipline is strong and is something the organization takes pride in.

What should the compensation be in such an organization? Let's start with the easy aspects. Expense accounts should be strictly controlled and should only apply to usual expenses: business travel, for instance, including fares, hotels and meals. These should be carefully defined so there are no excesses, which could get out of hand. In our firm they are restricted to so many dollars a day for meals and a comfortable hotel and — except for very long trips — economy fares. At all times, even-handedness and economy are the watchwords.

As for salaries, they should be fair to moderately generous. If you want an expert level of work, you should pay a better than adequate salary, but nothing extreme. Bonuses, where applicable, should be based on tough budgets and normally should not exceed 50% of salary (unless they are commission arrangements). Rarely, if ever, should they exceed 100% of salary. Salaries alone should provide a dignified standard of living, while annual bonuses supply the extras, whether luxury or savings.

Then there is long-term compensation (that is, beyond one year). This is essential so that key employees, over their careers, have the opportunity to grow alongside the company. With growth, capital appreciates, which is the reason shareholders invest. So top managers who can have a distinct influence on capital appreciation should share in the company's success over their working lives. Owning and retaining shares, being shareholders, is the ideal way to achieve this. Top managers should be material long-term shareholders, in proportion with their base salaries. Share purchase programs utilizing bonus funds are one way. Allocating rights to the appreciation of phantom shares, to be paid off at the time of retirement, or convertible to real shares at that time, is another. These executives and the shareholders then effectively share a common goal.

As mentioned, I greatly dislike most share option programs, especially those we have discussed earlier, which are normally exercised once vested and then sold the same week or month. Long-term compensation should not be a "bonus in disguise." Annual gifts of options to be sold immediately on being exercisable have been a main cause of the recent collapse of so many North American public corporations. If $1 per share appreciation is larger than an annual fair salary, it is no wonder that people will lie, cheat, and steal to get the stock price up, especially if the option can be exercised within a very short time limit.

The use of options should be highly controlled, when it is utilized at all. Options should be handed out only when someone receives a major promotion to a job where their effort is very important to the policy and development of the corporation. It should be a one-time option, and on vesting, it should be exercised only if the shares are held for the long term.

For people 50 and under, the holding period should be a minimum of 10 years, and the size of the option should be based on the salary level. The average stock grows some 4 to 6% over inflation annually. So over five years you can expect a minimum real gain of 20 to 30%. Assume this happens and you want this gain to equal two years' salary. Then the size of the options is fixed on that basis. The risk, of course, is that the outcome may be more or less than the average five-year gain. I emphasize again that the shares once issued should be kept long-term thereafter.

In many cases, however, option grants and their immediate sale on vesting have led to the looting of companies due to a major dilution of existing shareholders' equity. They have, worse yet, encouraged to excessive risk and excessive promotion, not to mention falsified accounts to artificially push up earnings and stock prices.

It is simply not necessary to issue options because share holdings can be developed in many other ways. I believe it is time to call a halt to 99% of the options now issued. They do not align management and shareholders, only management and stock market gamblers. We prefer the latter to use the casinos and leave only long-term shareholders as the true owners of our private economy. Options and their ilk have little place in companies with good management and a solid business culture. They only feed excessive greed and downgrade regular (that is, salary) compensation. They "lead people into temptation" too readily.

I once asked a bank president whether he would have resigned if his salary had been set at $600 000 plus a bonus of 50% maximum, instead of the $20 million he had reaped in the prior year. It took a bit of thought, but then he replied honestly that he had always hoped one day to be president and would not have stepped aside even without an extravagant salary. He didn't respond directly to my precise question, but it was clear to me that he genuinely wanted the experience of the job. Above all, it was the confidence of others that he would make a good president that appealed to him. This is the characteristic of a good executive, who, while ambitious, does not work in a vacuum but in an organization he loves and to which he feels a great responsibility beyond his own ego.

And so it should be. Top executives are not hockey players. They are mature adults who believe in things and values outside of themselves. They accept responsibility and believe that it is their job to carry it out in a way that earns the respect of both their employees and the community. How many of us are working for absolutely free for charity or community organizations? Most of us. There are also many of us who make major gifts to causes we believe in and stay around to assure that the money is well spent. A good executive considers himself a professional whose skill and knowledge is at the service of others.

I firmly believe that most top executives understand fully the role of fair compensation in a corporation, including their own. However, if a board wants to offer excessive compensation, not all are able to resist it — though I have met many who did. At SNC-Lavalin, the chief executive never felt that his compensation should exceed by too much that of his top lieutenants. He also felt that he should no longer be CEO after 65 and no longer be a director after 70. I agreed with the former, but not the latter. On the other hand, I had to deal with Conrad Black, who took absolutely exorbitant "management agreements" for himself and his henchmen in his holding company, often bypassing completely the company he supposedly worked for. We have seen where this has led his Lordship.

CEOs are entitled to receive a fair salary — one that is sufficient to provide a solid and comfortable style of life and take care of any worries about retirement. Their salary should also to some degree compensate their families for the sacrifices they must accept. But they should not receive salaries that detract from their dedication to the job. CEOs are not ordinary executives. They have to be on the scene all the time, seven days a week, 24 hours a day. Of course, it is possible to take some time off — even CEOs get vacations — but the company and its problems are always uppermost in their minds and must be tackled without delay. There are people who do not agree with me on this, but few top executives would take me to task.

If business targets are met or exceeded, CEOs should also be entitled to a bonus. When brought in new, or promoted to a position that has a major influence on the success of the company, an executive might also receive an option on shares proportional to the value of his or her salary. But this should not be excessive and should come with very definite strings attached to avoid abuse. The ultimate goal is to give CEOs a real stake in the company so that they will begin to think like actual shareholders and align their efforts with those who paid hard cash for their shares. This is what fair executive compensation should be all about.

Chapter 5

Directors:
Guardians or Lackeys?

The excesses we are witnessing in the corporate world today have been aided and abetted by company directors who have failed in their duty to protect the interests of investors — as well as by inaction on the part of large shareholders.

Small investors rely on these people — the boards of directors and more even on major shareholders — to look after their interests. The latter normally exercise no executive or board of director functions themselves. But large shareholders — especially those who have control of a corporation — can and possibly should be more involved. They should not leave the guardianship of shareholders' interests only to insiders, especially in a large public corporation.

They should nominate trusted and competent friends to the board of directors. They have too much at stake to simply leave it to management; they should assure that someone other than management looks after their interests. It is surprising that in so many corporations it is almost entirely management appointees who fill the boards, especially in companies where there is not a single major shareholder.

By law, a board of directors represents the shareholders and is elected by them each year. Modern boards normally have a nominating committee, which makes recommendations to assist in this process. Yet rare indeed is the occasion where shareholders make an attempt to add directors to the board.

The function of a board is to look after shareholders' interests by assuring that a company has a sound executive and operates effectively and ethically so as to produce the best long-term results. The board must look after every shareholder even-handedly, and each director, no matter what group may have installed him, should also look after all shareholders alike, big or small. But I have served on boards where the shareholder was rarely mentioned. The board, made up mainly of friends (cronies) of management, was normally there to do no more than rubber stamp the decisions of management, and the participation of many of the directors was pretty negligible.

Most company managements are quite happy to have directors who do not rock the boat. Often, an ex-politician or someone well connected in a region or country is asked to serve. All too often, a CEO is asked to serve on another company's board and so he asks the CEO of that company to reciprocate and serve on his board. "Birds of a feather flock together." Rarely is a representative of an investor group asked to serve and many institutional investors prefer not to, since this makes them an "insider" and may inhibit their freedom to buy and sell.

My partners traditionally have opposed my serving on boards of public companies, especially of companies in which we held shares. This is because the law prescribes that there be a Chinese wall between myself and our research and stock picking committees in order to avoid conflicts of interest. But I find this rather bizarre. My logic has always been that as an owner I should have a say.

I have been on many boards, but remained on the public ones only when the company had previously been private or when our firm felt (as was the case with Southam) that representation was imperative if we were not to get "ripped off" by the company and its board. I feel strongly that some of the governance problems we have been seeing stem from the fact that boards are either not even-handed or are in the pocket of management, or both.

At most board meetings I have attended, shareholders are rarely referred to and are seldom consulted about their wishes. Board members discussed issues related to financial statements and audits; senior appointments and compensation; budgets; and, in some cases, a strategic plan for the firm. The agenda also included capital expenditure approval, investments, and acquisitions. Dividend discussions were short and normally were based on management recommendations in view of cash requirements. Additional equity or financing matters were normally suggested by advisors or investment dealers. A director seldom made a proposal. It is no wonder that there are so many scandals and so much second-rate management. I would argue that this is the fault of the large institutional investors, who almost inevitably take no interest and allow their proxy vote to be used to simply endorse the "management slate" and support the "management resolutions."

It is not surprising that boards do not truly represent investors, if the large investors refuse to get involved, preferring instead to be free to buy and sell shares without ever having a "perceived conflict." Our firm has repeatedly asked other institutions to join us to oppose matters that are clearly against shareholder interest, only to be refused and see these firms give their proxy to management. This was either because it was their standing policy or because they did not want to alienate a management that might feed them business. In many cases our phone calls were never even answered by such firms. The mutual fund management companies were the worst; they seemed to prefer their suppliers of business over their clients.

So I would argue that many corporate scandals, many excessive salaries, bonuses, and options can be laid at the door of boards that in fact do not represent the shareholder interest. This in turn is largely the fault of the major institutional shareholders, who effectively control these companies and are the very shareholders who should insist that boards represent shareholders and not simply be puppets of management.

The rot in the corporations is effectively the fault of the large institutional investors who refuse to risk a conflict of interest when selling and buying. This in turn is echoed by the securities commissions and the lawmakers, who have made rules that perpetuate this kind of behaviour. How often are shareholder resolutions adopted? Almost never, although they surely would have some influence if they got 25% backing.

What the lawmakers and the institutions have forgotten is that the small shareholder is unable to enforce good governance. If the large investors abdicate their responsibility, it is obvious that the vacuum will be filled by management and its cronies — often other CEOs who have the same objective: to maximize the take.

Board members are on the front line, responsible for doing what is right and for remembering whom they represent. They should be honour bound to act in the interest of those for whom they are fiduciaries. That point in law is clear — but in practice few judges have been willing to challenge board decisions.

To try to improve this situation I, along with Claude Lamoureux, president and chief executive officer of the Ontario Teachers' Pension Plan, in 2002 decided to form the Canadian Coalition for Good Governance to fight for improved governance at Canadian companies. Our members now include 30 leading Canadian institutional investors with more than $600 billion in assets under management. They are the large shareholders of Canadian companies — those with voting power to influence governance practices that should benefit all shareholders. It is their task to assure the employ of committed directors and executives.

The goal of the coalition is to align the interest of boards and management with those of all shareholders and hold management accountable for increasing long-term shareholder value. We are doing this by monitoring the composition and performance of boards, sharing information on candidates to recommend to nominating committees, and insisting that key board committees have a majority of independent outside directors. We also will be working with securities commissions to strengthen regulations and with governments to introduce shareholder-friendly laws and to strengthen criminal penalties for abuse. In effect, we intend to be a catalyst for change in the best interests of many millions of Canadian investors.

In 2003, our coalition introduced 12 guidelines for Canada's largest publicly traded companies that propose minimum standards and best practices for company boards of directors to consider. These are focused on three areas: how individual directors of high quality are selected; how boards are structured to create team governance strengths; and how boards work to ensure good governance processes. We have also developed a self-appraisal form to help boards gauge their level of success in meeting the minimum governance standards set out by these guidelines.

As far as we know, we are the only such coalition in the world. There are other organizations that basically say, "Here are the guidelines we recommend." We take this one step further and say, "We want to discuss how you can improve your governance, and at the end of the day, if we're unhappy, we always have the option to vote our shares against you." We speak softly, but we carry a big stick!

Sadly, many directors today seek to shirk their responsibilities by buying liability insurance. Who pays for it? The corporation, of course. But why should a fiduciary not be personally liable if he betrays his trust? Why should shareholders pay a director if he forgets to do his duty? Personally, I have never felt a need to be protected by such insurance. As a director, I must do my duty with regard to the shareholders while acting in the best legitimate interests of the corporation.

My job is to ensure that management is excellent and, if not, to make changes. If management is excellent it should be fairly compensated — no more, no less! Products should be good, because consumers are entitled to quality. The customer should be happy and, if not, that should be addressed. Employee working conditions should be safe and reliable. Salaries and wages should be appropriate, and exceptional effort and achievement should be recognized. The company should be a good citizen in the community in which it operates, but not a Santa Claus nor paternalistic. Accounting should be accurate and conservative . Finances should at all times protect the shareholders' equity. Expansion should be well thought through and never exorbitant. Unprofitable divisions should be straightened out or be disposed of if they can't be fixed. There should be teamwork, good morale, and a minimum of politics. I'm not in favour of prima donnas. There should be no ego trips and no gambling. Budgets should be demanding, but feasible. And so forth.

The contribution of directors should be reviewed and discussed with them on a regular basis. Being a director should not be an honorific sinecure, but a service to the company and its shareholders. Yes, there should be director's fees, but not so high that a director might think twice before resigning. Yes, directors should hold shares in the company. But the amounts should be reasonable and proportional to the director's net worth — neither too few nor too many shares. Directors should be knowledgeable. They should have backgrounds in accounting or human relations if they are to serve on the audit or the human resources committee. They should know the major assets, physical and human. Through presentations, dinners, lunches, etc., they should meet most of the decision makers in management. Plant visits are important to get a feel for efficiency and morale. I have resisted the use of outside consultants on boards, except for technical problems that are beyond the scope of the knowledge and expertise of our own people.

I believe that the auditors should report directly and exclusively to the board and that the board should set their mandate. Auditors must do more than make sure that accepted accounting procedures are followed. They must make sure that the statements are conservative and can be taken by shareholders as correct and reliable. If not, what is the point of having an outside auditor?

I believe that the human resources committee is the most important board agent, as it assures the quality of both present management and future development, as well as determines fair but not excessive compensation. The CEO's salary should not be far out of line with that of his top lieutenants; top management must be able to work as a group with a minimum of politics and infighting caused by envy and desire for the top job.

I strongly feel that the points I am raising here are in the interest of the shareholders and that these are some of the things that fiduciaries should be responsible for keeping track of.

The size of a company's board also matters. It should be composed of no more directors than are needed to fill the important committees and provide a balanced view from people with different strengths and areas of knowledge. Normally, a board of eight to ten people strikes me as the right number for a large company, while six to eight are enough for a smaller or simpler company. My company has seven directors.

Board meetings should take a morning or an afternoon — or at most all day when something major like a new strategic plan is discussed. The basic information and formalities probably take half that time, leaving some two hours for discussion and questions. With too many board members, there is too little time for real participation. If you have 30 directors, for instance, each one would have just four minutes to ask questions and receive answers, including time for discussion. That clearly makes no sense.

Board matters frequently require lengthy discussions to arrive at the best decision. These should not be cut short or, worse, muzzled. Board discussions should be open and incisive, and staff should be prepared to provide both the information that directors may desire and answers to tough questions. Boards must insist that management do its homework and that board requests are responded to with logic and solid facts.

I further believe that there should be a "lead director," and that the chairman should not be the chief executive. That makes sense, because the agenda should be the board's and not the CEO's. The chairman, as well as the entire board, should be regarded by the CEO and any other management people as mentors of the company. They are people with enormous experience and talent and absolute integrity. The board is the final authority and there should be no doubt in anyone's mind whether it is, in fact, a strong board. If it isn't, you don't have the right directors.

A strong board is actually quite fun; it functions on mutual respect and admiration. A strong board has a great sense of integrity and keeps the shareholders' interest foremost — but not the shareholders' greed. A good board observes the golden mean between extremes: It balances the shareholders' desire for greater wealth with the reality of what good management can produce with an acceptable risk. If a company is well-managed, depending on its industry and the overall economy, there is a certain rate of growth that is achievable safely over the long term. This is what a good board aims for.

I personally do not feel that a board should be involved in the share price or its promotion. Rather, the markets should take care of share price, based on such factors as a company's earnings, dividends, and growth. If prices rise too high or fall too low by wide margins, some comment can be made, but only as advice to shareholders with little knowledge. Curb greed and curb panic — simply that. If the shares are in a normal range, the price deserves no comment. If shares are cheap, shareholders have an opportunity to acquire more. If in the high range, they can take some profit.

Shareholder information should be forthright regarding favourable and unfavourable factors; recurrent earnings should be published and special pluses or minuses pointed out. The company should have a definite and well-communicated dividend policy. I believe in fair and full disclosure, but not excessive information that might confuse.

Annual reports, for example, should be simple and concise for the average shareholder, not a maze of legal and accounting "gobbledegook" that even a qualified analyst could not make heads or tails of. I detest the type of annual report that lists only achievement and brushes failures under the carpet. I have read many glowing reports of companies that went bust within 12 months! Moreover, approval of the annual report, quarterly reports, press releases, and other shareholder documents are board matters. They should be signed and released by the chairman of the board after board approval. This should not be left to management alone, as it is the board that is the representative of the shareholders.

It's also important that a director act as a trustee for all shareholders alike. If there is a large shareholder, it is the outside directors' role to make sure this person does not use his or her position oppressively or unfairly. If you look at companies like Weston and Thomson, it is clear that these companies are run in the proper manner. Others that I can cite are not, and I believe that intelligent investors should avoid them, even if that gives a chance to the oppressing shareholder to buy shares on the cheap.

This kind of company should be exposed, and the regulatory authorities should take action to put a stop to this sort of oppression. Jarislowsky Fraser has often brought before the courts companies in which boards were merely pals of the owner. We have very often failed to win our case, however, as the courts only too frequently refuse to go against a board of directors' decision. As fiduciaries, true directors should act professionally. They have knowledge and power that most shareholders do not. And like any professional whom clients rely on for knowledge and expertise, a director has a duty to put the client's interest first.

It is unfortunate that many professionals do not follow this rule. Just as the unethical actions of some lawyers tend to taint the public image of all practitioners — even those who are highly ethical — so the behaviour of some board members puts all boards in bad odour with the public. Boards of major companies need to reform and become true trustees for the shareholders. And institutional investors must learn to exercise — or be coerced to exercising — the power that already rests in their hands to assure good boards and good corporate governance. They must put aside their conflicts of interest and work for those for whom they are fiduciaries — the clients — not the agent who brings them the clients.

Lawmakers and securities watchdogs also have an important role to play in protecting the interests of small shareholders. I believe very firmly that if the shareholders are to be protected, securities commissions should make recommendations to the lawgivers to promote the making of more appropriate laws. That's one reason why we set up the Canadian Coalition for Good Governance. And the more deeply we investigate this, the more we find that the existing laws completely fail to protect shareholders in Canada.

Sadly, our current securities commissions are not acting to protect shareholders. Their main activity seems to be creating mountains of paperwork by making regulations that require the filling out of forms by everybody and his brother and the annual filing of countless trivial documents, including the preparation of prospectuses that nobody's really interested in and nobody can read because they are written in legal gibberish. This represents an enormous amount of work and cost without anything practical being achieved — certainly not the protection of shareholders or the public.

Clearly, investors are operating in a jungle with some very vicious animals. And these vicious animals know that anybody who is stupid enough to hand money over to them is prey. Investors can go to people like us at Jarislowsky Fraser or the Canadian Coalition for Good Governance, but even we cannot fully protect them. The laws permit these shenanigans to be legally perpetrated; and when we point the problems out to the securities commissions, all they say is, "It's legal; we can't do anything." So investors are in trouble. To my mind, it is the responsibility of the commissions and commissioners to point this out to the lawmakers and get the laws changed.

The Canadian system of protecting shareholders with regard to takeovers, going private, and insider trading is totally biased against shareholders. Majority owners can buy out the minority without paying a fair price. This injustice has to be studied and the legislation brought up to date, with specialized arbitration boards assigned to hear cases rather than the courts. Dual-class shares should have sunset clauses that see multiple-voting shares convert into common stock in the event of a takeover. And penalties for securities violations must be tougher. I also believe we need a single Canadian securities regulator — one with more power than the current provincial commissions have.

I'm an advocate of investing in individual stocks, but investors have to always be on their guard because of our lax securities regulations. The shareholder is currently the bottom person on the totem pole. Everybody gets fed before him — the banks, the labour unions, the tax department, the lawyers, the accountants, and the executives. If there's anything left, then maybe it goes to the shareholder. It's a very sad scene.

What has happened is that everybody but the investors has had major input into formulating and changing securities laws and bringing about remediation. And then, even if you go to court and your case is good, most judges will say, "Well, I don't know as much as the board of directors so I am not going to challenge their decisions." As a result, we have misdeeds like those perpetrated by the empire of Conrad Black, and others like Enron and WorldCom. One can't help but wonder also about the competence of the judges who deal with shareholder cases.

Too often the laws and the deep pockets favour the corporations rather than the investor. And once they have the minority investor's money, they see him or her as merely a nuisance. Moreover, the laws and regulations are highly influenced by both the corporate and financial sectors — and their well-paid lawyers. For the most part, the securities commissioners are nowhere to be seen. They rarely act based on overriding principles of fairness and ethics. If something isn't clearly proven to be illegal, a call to the regulator is a futile gesture. In the few cases where the commissions have acted, their comparatively ill-paid lawyers have been no match for the high-paid lawyers of the predators— who are also able to drag the process out interminably. Justice postponed indefinitely is justice denied.

The judicial process needs a major overhaul to be really effective and ethical. And if there is one case that demonstrates how badly reform is needed, it is the KeepRite case: millions of dollars in lawyers fees, a saga that went on for years, and a judge who, because he could "not prove beyond the shadow of a doubt that the directors had done anything wrong," aligned himself with the company rather than protect the shareholders. It was possibly the most blatant case of oppression I have ever been involved in. We basically lost the case, and to this day I do not know whether the judge, who blindly backed the board of directors, ever really thoroughly understood the issues.

A very prominent member of KeepRite's board, Purdy Crawford (dean of the Toronto legal establishment at the time and a friend now), had warned me that I would lose. The case was heard before an Ontario judge. As the plaintiffs were essentially Quebec residents, we appealed, but the Ontario Court of Appeal upheld the trial judge 100%. The cost of the eight-year trial was astronomical. And my faith in courts giving justice was badly shaken. But then I remembered reading, in the work of the French satirist Rabelais, about his hero Pantagruel becoming judge of Lyons. Pantagruel became famous as the most expedient and fair judge in France: To decide who would win the case, he tossed a coin!

One of the only times the Ontario Securities Commission (OSC) has actually stood up was in the attempted Canadian Tire Corporation takeover. The issue was the enormous discrepancy between what would be paid for the common shares (multiple-voting) and the category A (subordinated) shares. A number of people, including Stanley Beck, the chairman of the OSC and a former Dean of Osgoode Hall Law School at York University, and myself, mounted a vigorous protest against this gross inequity. For once the OSC took it upon itself to rule that the deal was totally unfair. We were subsequently able to elect to the board a director of our choice, my good friend Ron Oberlander, who later became president and chairman of Abitibi-Consolidated. He did a splendid job at Canadian Tire and gained the admiration of all, including Martha Billes, the holder of the control block. Since that time, Canadian Tire has become a model of good governance, despite having two classes of shares.

We were also involved in a similar case much earlier with the Supertest Petroleum Corporation, a chain of service stations. Shell Oil, which wanted to buy Supertest, offered a ridiculous price for the multiple-voting shares owned by the Thompson family. In the 1960s, together with the Jackmans, a prominent Toronto business family, we fought this unfair arrangement and won major modifications in the final deal.

Over the years we have fought many such takeover attempts. In most we did everything we could to come to a fair value understanding with the buyer rather than go to court. One of the cases we were not able to settle out of court is now quite famous. In 1978, Consolidated-Bathurst, a Power Corporation subsidiary, took control of Domglas, offering minority shareholders, we among their number, $20 a share for their stake in Domglas. We did not believe this was a fair price and contested it. The case was heard in Montreal in 1980 and our lawyer, François Mercier, won it hands down. Quebec's Superior Court ruled that Consolidated-Bathurst should pay $36 rather than $20 a share to the minority shareholders. This case remains a classic in Canadian and Quebec law books.

François and I were celebrating our victory at the Mount Royal Club on Sherbrooke Street when Paul Desmarais, the controlling shareholder of Power Corp., walked in. I chided him for not congratulating us, which he then graciously did, asking François why he had worked for us. François's reply: "You didn't ask me to represent you!" Good fun and games in the end — but also a reflection of the often mercenary nature of our business.

Chapter 6

The Investment Business: *caveat emptor*!

With corporate greed running rampant, directors shirking their responsibilities, and ineffective securities laws, shareholders rightly feel that the stock market may only too often be a rigged game. "Why did we ever buy stocks or mutual funds?" New scandals and poor earnings reports do not help — they only increase public distaste for stocks and explain the flight to more consumption (why save if you cannot invest in proper growth?) or new housing (at least I own it and live in it).

The problem is that most people who have little investment experience do not know where to turn or what to buy. Not being knowledgeable, they either pick up "tips" from friends or they work with a stockbroker or financial advisor. Those who act on tips are "flying on a wing and a prayer" and don't know when to get out. Stockbrokers and investment advisors, for their part, too often have their own interests, not those of their clients, uppermost in their minds.

Few people tip Abbott Laboratories, Philip Morris, or General Electric. You'd be more likely to hear a name like Bre-X — which turned out to be a pretty volatile thing! Of course there are exceptions, but chances are if you listen to five tips, no more than one of them will be a solid, long-term choice. The public, by and large, looks at the stock market as a place little different from a casino. Unfortunately, the result is often similar —except that in the casino you lose or win more rapidly. But on net, you are going to be a long-term loser.

Brokers make their money on commissions. So if an investor worked with a broker and bought Abbott Laboratories, the poor sap would make one commission in a lifetime, unless the client had new money to place. But even then there would only be buying, no selling. It doesn't make much sense for a broker to sterilize money for 40 years. So he gets you to buy what is popular at the time and sell when you make 20%. He will tell you that you "never lose money taking a profit," or if you are down from cost, he has a "smart switch" or a "better bet" for you. Of course, he gets commissions each time!

One man with common sense asked his broker, "Why aren't you rich, if you are so smart?" Only a broker who is rich can afford to give advice without needing commissions. But there are very few who don't like to show their partners how much they earned in commissions this month. The reality is, commissions cost the investor money. The more you trade, the less chance you have to make a return, unless you are big enough and clever enough not to get caught when you "rig the market." If the average return on stocks over 100 years is 5 to 6% per annum, don't spend 5 to 6% in commissions!

I could earn $1 million a year as a witness for shareholders who believe they were ripped off by brokers and underwriters. I am not always sure that investors' greed didn't also enter the picture, but there is no doubt that most brokers are judged by the commissions they bring in rather than by how well their clients do.

This conflict of interest is inherent in the investment business. The naive logical answer is that brokers should, like investment counsel, work for a flat percentage over the year with no specific commissions on trades, or should simply not be allowed to solicit orders or give advice.

But for now, every dollar that a broker, dealer or investment advisor earns comes out of the funds of investors. So of course do corporate salaries, wages, and the money for bankers, lawyers, accountants, and the tax department. I could go on for a long time… Workers, executives, and others who run the corporations we invest in are, of course, essential — only how much they are paid is really at issue, not whether they should be paid. Provided that these people are fairly paid, their salaries are a normal cost of doing business.

But there are so many "costs of doing business" and investor fees come in many forms: As discussed above, the broker gets paid a commission every time the investor buys or sells. Similarly, shareholders have to pay the underwriter, the necessary intermediary between them and the company offering the shares. Investment counsel fees (paying a flat fee over the year for investment advice) may help clients to make more money, but here too there are times when clients end up with less by taking their counsellor's advice than if they just kept their holding at the start. Custodian fees may be a necessary evil, especially in pooled or mutual funds, but they too diminish the shareholder return. And the reality is that financial advisor fees and mutual fund management and sales fees — just like brokers' commissions — come straight out of the investors' wallets.

Trading leads to commissions, ergo the less you trade the less you pay for that function. Clearly for investors, all things being equal, the fewer fees you pay the more your total wealth is maintained. But investors who are making trades and dealing with a stockbroker would be well-advised to negotiate the commission — as is now common practice. If you do not negotiate, you may end up paying up to 2% commission on each trade; whereas if you use a discount broker, you may pay no more than 0.1 to 0.3%. What a difference!

Stockbrokers typically are remunerated only through commissions. At the end of the year, they must have made enough trades to survive. They are not normally judged by how well you, the investor, does — only by what their annual commissions add up to. And low-priced stocks usually earn them more than high-priced ones.

On a sale of a mutual fund, as long as the broker keeps you in it, he may be paid 0.5% of the purchase value each year, even if it is a "bum" fund. And if he buys you a gambling stock, chances are you will trade it, since in the long term it is not a safe, dividend-paying investment. It is often not an investment at all — only a gamble, no different from a bet placed at the casino. If, instead, you bought Coca-Cola or Pfizer, you could keep the stock for years and years, get higher dividends, and pay no further commissions at all.

Brokers typically will appeal to your greed instincts. That means speculative securities, many of which are temporarily fashionable darlings, sure to crash once the love affair is over. WorldCom, Nortel, and Tyco are some of the highest-profile examples of this we've seen recently.

New issues typically are well promoted. To be sure, every successful company was launched at some point. But my experience is that you can buy nine out of ten new issues at a lower price a year or two later. Companies usually go public only when they can get a high price at outset, unless they are badly in need of quick money for one reason or another. Because of this, I generally avoid new issues, only very occasionally buying one as an exception. I have not always been right, and some that I passed on I should have grabbed. But all told this policy has saved me enormous pain. Just think of all the dot com and high-tech new issues — now largely defunct companies or equally worthless. The lesson: Do not buy fashionable securities; all fashions go out, none lasts long!

Investment dealers also distribute secondary issues — that is, stock that is already issued that the owner wishes to sell a large block of without killing the market. Again, normally these transactions are carried out when the stock is high, but not always. Some blocks are offered to allow the seller to diversify. Frequently an organization like a family foundation will take this step. These blocks may be of interest, but make sure the company is still sound and growing and that the price is reasonable — and not at an all-time high.

We've all read about scandals in the mutual fund industry related to a practice known as "juicing." This unsavoury practice is again driven by greed and further adds to small investor mistrust of the markets. Many fund managers and analysts get an incentive pay package. So analysts for fund managers often get a big bonus if their stocks outperform the sub-index for that section or the S&P/TSX Composite Index. No outperformance, no bonus. So what can analysts do to get a bonus if their stocks are underperforming? They buy a few more shares of those stocks with limited marketability. And they buy "at the market." But since often there is little offered, they grab whatever is available and the price gets higher. That helps their valuation and eureka! Instant bonus!

Any large manager can manipulate stocks in this way. In our firm there are many smaller companies of which we hold almost 20% of the public shares. If we placed a market order for these smaller companies for, say, 50 000 shares, we could raise the price 10 to 20% because of their small trading floats. Such a company might normally trade only 2000 shares a day. The only reasonable way to accumulate this kind of stock is to place an open order at a certain price, preferably under the market, and then pray that someone is eager to sell. That way you would avoid overpaying — but this strategy would not help your performance. Placing a large market order will clean out all the offers, low and high.

If you have lots of broker friends you could even get them to tout a stock as a "sell," while buying it up yourself, and then, when you have your position, ask them to tout it as a "strong buy," allowing you to sell all the stock you've accumulated — at a better price than you bought it for, of course. I remember one mutual fund manager who was an expert at this game in days gone by.

The practice of "juicing" is just plain cheating. But surveillance, regulation, and punishment have been completely lacking. In fact, we should ask where the securities commissions have been in all this. Have the crooks that perpetrated the Bre-X theft been brought to justice? I don't know of one behind bars.

Where have the securities commissions been in the rape of the investor by options and greed that saw completely falsified statements put forth to keep the momentum going and options more valuable? Was the $1 million penalty against Michael Cowpland's holding company really a deterrent — given that he had sold for $20 million at a big profit when he knew the stock might collapse?

The securities commissions have not given guidance to investors or sounded the alarm at the pilfering of corporations. In reality, they should insist that the option dilution be squarely put in the income statement and on the balance sheet. The Cinar, Livent, and Enron cases could very probably been avoided. And as for the accountants, there seems to be good reason to mistrust them. One could ask why, for instance, the auditor reports to the board when he is really paid by management and so may be in cahoots with them. Auditors should be required to pronounce on the integrity of the statements, not merely to confirm that they conform with standard accounting practice, a practice that lets the auditor completely off the hook. To me an auditor should be a watchdog. Why else do I need him? I already have accountants on the payroll!

I am equally suspicious of mutual fund salespeople and financial advisors. Again I would want to know how rich they are and how they make their money. Mutual fund salespeople are often stockbrokers who turned to selling mutual funds because their competitively low commissions didn't allow them to make a living selling just stocks. And financial advisors are only too often just mutual fund and insurance salespeople in disguise.

I am not part of the current mutual fund vogue, which through slick advertising sucks in all kinds of small, unsophisticated investors. Forget, for a moment, the front-end and exit load funds and just look at the operating costs — which are usually in small print and not even put in context. Assume that the average mutual fund (and there are as many as there are stock market listings) earns the 100-year average return in stocks of an annual 5 to 6%. Now if your operating costs plus commissions absorb 2%, you take all the risk for a 3 to 4% average real return, and this is eventually taxable even in a deferred tax plan.

Thus between 33 and 40% of your return after inflation, but before tax, goes to the manager. In many instances, including the case of front-end loads, Canadian mutual funds take more than 2% per year. If you have a broker, chances are the mutual fund also pays him 0.5 to 0.75% per year just to make sure you don't sell the fund, so that they can all continue to feast on you. So be sure to really know what your total cost is. Our firm never takes more than 0.5% for specialized management of private accounts. It is true that normally we do not take accounts under $1 000 000, but that is our maximum fee and for large accounts it can go down to 0.1%. If the average stock compounds at 5 to 6% real (above inflation), the difference of 1.5% in long-term compounding is enormous — just test it yourself.

Simply put, most mutual funds are very expensive, with up to half your expected long-term gain siphoned off in fees at no risk to anyone but you. Exit fees may further materially reduce your take, especially on losing funds, as the fees are computed on your purchase cost, not on the value of the fund when you sell it. In a bull market mutual funds may make sense — but in a bear or flat market these are usually poor vehicles. True, the fund managers make more money if you make more money, but their management fees are so high that, given the long-term return, they constitute too much of a risk. By comparison, long-term quality bonds (those with a 10 year maturity or longer) give you 2% real return with very low risk, provided you don't cash them in before maturity. If you do, however, you will end up with a negative return on bonds after inflation and tax.

Mutual fund managers who can create good performance are well rewarded. And not only in financial terms: Their funds sell better as consultants point out that they lead the parade. They're talked about in the newspapers and on television. If they are lucky their photos appear in ads daily. Temporarily they become heroes! Mutual fund competition is like war, and "all's fair in love and war."

The various misdeeds of investment dealers are discouraging to investors, since in the end it is the investors' property that is reduced by these greedy practices. But if investors lose confidence, there will be fewer jobs, less prosperity, and a pervasive distrust of our capitalist system. That would be a severe setback for the economies of the world!

Whether you are a big or small investor, it is time to speak up. Do not allow your trust company or investment dealer to blindly sign management's proxy. In many cases it is these proxies automatically sent in that carry the day. Let's have a law that these proxies must be sent to the real owners for signing and mailing. Also let us forbid by law the incentives that companies pay brokers to send in shares or proxies. These amount to nothing more than simple bribes, as these fancy proxies are inevitably used for management's purposes.

Let's also forbid the "trailer fees" paid to brokers by mutual funds to keep investors in their shares. This often results in people being tricked into keeping a poor investment. After all, if the investment were good, there would be no need for a bribe to sway the broker.

Taking into account the practices described above and the recent scandals that have rocked the world of high finance, is it any wonder that very few small private investors do well? It is time for investors to snap out of their apathy, stop being taken advantage of, and start seriously defending their interests. To do this investors need knowledge — enough knowledge to be buyers rather than be sold a bill of goods.

Small investors may also consider buying in-house mutual funds (Phillips, Hager & North has a successful one). In doing so, they get good investment counsel while avoiding astronomical management fees. Fees for in-house funds are generally well below 2.5% and normally there are no other charges. A conservative, well-diversified fund with a fee of 1.25% or lower can make good sense. Investment counsel, as well, is typically only accessible to people with considerable portfolios ($500 000 and over). And I would recommend that here too you look carefully at the fees being charged and investigate thoroughly the quality of services being offered by the firm before you sign.

At 0.5% annually the rates at Jarislowsky Fraser are without a doubt among the lowest in the sector. And a fee difference of even 0.5% or 0.25% compounded makes quite a difference over 10 to 20 years. Assuming again the 5 to 6% real long-term return rates for stocks, whether you pay 0.5% or 1% in fees annually translates to roughly a 10% difference in your net. Your interests and those of your investment counsel are similar. The more your money grows, the greater his reward. Avoid fees that have a premium for results, unless you like gambling. Higher returns may mean more risk for you — and it is your funds at risk, not the investment manager's. Be sure that your risk profile is lined up with his. You risk losing your capital while he, at worst, only gets a lower fee.

Custodians are necessary, unless you want to run to your safety deposit box whenever you make a trade. But they can be costly, especially if you do a lot of trading. However, the large brokers will usually hold your securities, as that way they can count on your trades. Their commissions may be a bit higher than the discount brokers', but this arrangement can save you a lot of time and effort checking up on dividend receipts and other documentation. If you do not trade much, this can be a good arrangement.

My basic conclusion is that it is supremely important to minimize the expense of investing, since each annual 0.25% makes a big difference over a 20-year period. Adopting a strict, disciplined, high-quality investment philosophy requiring few trades goes a long way in that direction and allows you to sleep well and get through panicky periods in the market easily. Typically, you should avoid new issues and any expensive products such as mutual funds with high management fees. If you have sufficient means, use top-quality investment counsel and, if not, look for their low-cost in-house mutual funds and choose balanced (stocks and bonds) or high-quality equity funds.

It is very important for an investor to choose a money manager who is not only knowledgeable but also ethical. There is a limit to performance expectation unless you are willing to take a lot of risk. Do not be dazzled by rising "stars." Rather, stick with funds where decisions are based on sound long-term policies and good research. Don't sell them when they have a bad year or two — this happens even to the best. If their choices and policies are good, you will get good longer-term results with low risk to your capital.

As long as investors are guided by greed and consultants find it hard to resist recommending funds that feed that greed, there will be managers who stray from the straight and narrow. Finally, look at how fund managers and analysts are rewarded. If they get enormous short-term performance bonuses, *caveat emptor* (let the buyer beware).

Chapter 7

Investing
in the Jungle

There are many ways to make money in investments. There are also numerous ways to waste your time — or worse, lose money. And losing money is inevitably easier than making money!

Remember that if you invest badly from the start, chances are you will continue to do so. So it's critical to have a good investment plan very early on and to stick to your plan.

Money over a lifetime is best made by the principle of compound growth. Start early, and try to choose investments of minimum risk, but which have a chance to double every five to seven years.

Compound growth is a well-known investment concept. The rules are simple: If your investments generate an average 14% annual return, they will double every five years. The benefits are startling: Over a 40-year work period (age 25 to age 65), you can turn $100 000 into $25.6 million. If your investments generate a 10% annual average return, they will double every seven years. The $100 000 will then grow to "just" $5.1 million over a 40-year period. No doubt you will be surprised by the difference. This underlines the fact that you must start saving early and then invest right. Major errors are very costly.

Let me put the compound growth effect another way. Assume you have $100 000 to invest by age 40 after you have bought your home, car, and perhaps a cottage. Again, assume that your money doubles every five years (a very ambitious target but not an unrealistic goal). From age 40 to age 60 you will push the $100 000 to $1.6 million. However, had you started with only $10 000 at age 20, by age 60, as seen before, this sum alone would have grown to $2.6 million. If you had been lucky enough to have $100 000 at age 20, you could have reached $25.6 million rather than the $1.6 million you could have made starting at age 40.

So why not forgo that second car, or pay rent before getting stuck with a huge mortgage, and start investing at age 20? I gave each of my four children $50 000 when they reached 18. If we succeed with the compound growth principle, each will have accumulated $12 million or more by the age of 60. So I maintain that even if you only achieve a fraction of that gain, the idea of an early start is absolutely essential.

Unfortunately, most people do just the opposite. Instead of putting aside money when young, they believe that they will never grow old and can spend what they make and carry whatever debt the bank or leasing company will allow. This is, of course, the road to eventual slavery and a terrible old age. And it can be easily prevented by a little forethought. All that is necessary is to begin investing early in life and have a basic understanding of compound growth.

Once your initial plan is underway, anything you earn later can be far more readily spent, since once you have sown the seeds of a good investment plan, compound growth will take care of the rest. Why this is not taught in high school I will never understand, because it is far simpler than most of the things — totally useless later — that you have to absorb and regurgitate in class.

However, I must emphasize again: Just saving money and putting it in the bank, into a house, into any stock, etc. will not do. You must link your capital to investments with a predictable rate of compound growth.

So what type of investment can best allow compound growth to work for you?

I am an advocate of investing in individual, high-quality stocks, provided you take care to avoid certain pitfalls. Historically, stocks have proven to offer as good a return as any other investment vehicle — and nothing I've seen over the past 50 years of investing has shaken my faith in stocks.

As a general rule, I'm opposed to relying on real estate as a way to achieve acceptable compound growth. Real estate is a highly cyclical industry. It may experience bursts of rapidly increasing prices, as we've seen in Canada and the US in recent years. But once the frenzy stops, the "slippery slope" begins and prices may decline sharply — as many Quebecers discovered during the days of the "separatist threat."

If the price of houses continually rose faster than the rate of inflation and growth in the gross national product (GNP), it is obvious that after a while very few people would be able to afford them. In addition, houses are assets with liabilities such as mortgage interest, taxes, utilities, repairs, and insurance. I'm not saying that you shouldn't own a house, or even, if you're wealthy enough, a country home as well. But it must be acknowledged that they involve a lot of overhead. At least with stocks and bonds, you never have to go out and shovel the snow! And it can often be cheaper to rent, especially in markets where houses are vastly overpriced.

In areas where population and wealth are rapidly expanding and top-quality recreational and other land is very scarce (and real estate tax is low), land could well be a superb investment. I'm thinking of waterfront in British

Columbia, say, one hour north of the major development thrust on Vancouver Island. Top recreational land (unless in national parks) eventually takes value. But these opportunities are hard to come by.

Some investment counsellors, the self-described "gold bugs," promote gold as a wise investment choice. But to me, gold is a symbol of fear that reaps few benefits over time. Gold has not kept pace with inflation for the past 60 to 70 years. It goes up and down and produces no income. If you had bought $35 US worth of gold in 1932, it would now be worth around $400 US. I can assure you that $35 in 1932 bought a hell of a lot more merchandise than $400 can buy today. In the meantime, you would have had no return whatsoever. Gold does not appeal to me except in the form of jewellery to be enjoyed.

Collecting art can be a good investment but requires a very sharp eye and in-depth knowledge. Take top-quality Chinese art today. China is becoming capitalist and more and more millionaires are being created there, leading to rising values for local artworks. The ancient art supply is obviously limited, since "they don't make it anymore." And no doubt quality jade, bronze, ceramics, paintings, and antique furniture will also begin to take on greater and greater value. As far as contemporary art goes, if you have a great eye and can spot the next Monet, Van Gogh, or David Milne, you may effect doubling in five years. These collectibles do not pay dividends, so no tax is paid till you declare a capital gain. But obviously such artworks are out of reach of the average investor and so are not a realistic option for most.

Bonds may have a place in your investment portfolio but are not very appealing over the long term. They provide very low returns if "safe," and if not safe, you don't know what you're getting and can risk losing it all. Under most circumstances, if they are subject to tax, bonds do not generate a material real return. If non-taxable, a bond yielding 5% will generate a real return of only 3% after accounting for 2% inflation. You're clearly not going to get rich on 3%, and it will take a very long time for your money to double.

Moreover, in the last century, common stocks have outperformed bonds in any 25-year period since such statistics have been kept — that is, in any period from 1925 to 2000. I have no doubt that this record continues today.

So that leaves us with stocks, which I continue to believe represent the best way to maximize compound growth. But how do you find the right ones?

I've always viewed the stock market as a place that provides you with a chance to buy superb investments. It also gives you a chance to be a good human being: to make someone happy who wants to buy at the top and to help someone out who never wants to see their stocks again! If you do that, you will have become a true professional since the idea is to "buy cheap, sell dear."

Some may say that anything is worth buying if the price is low enough. However, my rule is to invest only in top-quality, largely non-cyclical growth stocks that have a predictable high rate of earnings and, hopefully, dividend growth. I believe that if you keep this in mind, you will stay on track. Then there is no reason to be confused and overwhelmed by all the stocks (like stars) that are out there.

A good investor has the courage to make choices. The stock market is a bit like a zoo. There are all kinds of animals there, from elephants to tigers to snakes to monkeys. You only need a few of the best species to build a good diversified portfolio that will provide sustainable, low-risk, high compound earnings. All you need to do is find them, buy them at reasonable prices, and make sure they stay on track. So how should you go about this?

Needless to say, stock investment can be a confusing business. When you look at the stock pages in the financial section of a newspaper you'll see thousands of stocks listed. Some sell at $100 per share, others sell for pennies.. Some pay dividends, many pay none. All represent companies trying to make a profit, but peruse the earnings reports in the paper and you'll also note that many companies seem to lose money. I have wondered how they stay alive. When I consider the small number of shares that interest me after 50 years of following stocks, I ask who owns all these other companies and, more importantly, why?

Considering that there are so few important mines, you have to query who owns all the other mining ventures. And why would some of these companies have gone public in the first place? They have paltry sales and few prospects and are totally controlled by promoters drawing salaries. I have rarely seen even small capitalization stock funds that would go near them with a "ten foot pole." Are these only poker chips rather than stocks? Are they just "sucker bait"? Why would anyone spend their hard earned savings on most of the stocks that are listed on the market? No rational, logical investor that I know, able to calculate odds, would touch them. So it must be innocent or gullible people who invest without using their brains, or who are "sold" glints of riches by unscrupulous salespeople.

So which stocks should you buy? The first point to remember if you want to become a sensible investor is to eschew emotions, especially greed and fear. Don't fall in love; go no further than friendship. Keep things "Platonic" — that is, rational!

The second point is to forget for a while about what the stock market does as a whole and concentrate just on the companies you own shares in. One pundit has said he invests as if he were the owner of the whole company. If it company does well, in time he will become wealthy, even if he only owns a small percentage of the shares. There are, after all, many private companies, never listed on a market, whose owners have become very rich indeed.

The stock market day-to-day is like the ocean: sometimes calm, sometimes stormy. But all you see is the surface not what goes on below. On the superficial level, it is subject to crazes in any direction; the average stock has a 30% value swing in one year. Clearly, real underlying values don't change that much

— but the "herd's" perception does. One year gold is all the rage; the next it is junior oil stocks or real estate empires. In the short term, the market simply mirrors greed and fear, and the perceptions emanating from these two emotions. In the long term, however, it manifests growth "on average," reflecting the performance of the companies that continue to grow, earn more, and pay ever higher dividends. But if you look at the charts for the stocks that make up the S&P (Standard & Poor's) 500 index over 10 years, you will be able to discern very little correlation between the performance of individual stocks and the overall market trend.

I have never met anyone who has predicted the stock market consistently or accurately. All the great seers of the past have eventually bitten the dust. The chance of being right is 50% the first time, and by the time you made a second prediction, it falls to 25%. Thus any mathematician will tell you the odds are against you! There are just too many factors at work — many of them completely illogical — for anyone to be able to build a model. I conclude from this that no one really knows what markets will do. Similarly, in the short term (unless you manipulate a stock, which is illegal), there are just too many buyers and sellers for it to be possible to accurately predict the action of a specific stock. Earnings news, external events, and people's perceptions of future profits are all elements that are hard — or impossible — to control. Even as a director of public companies, my short-term prediction record has never been anything to brag about.

So I am not a believer in market timing. Nor do I feel that I really possess absolute knowledge of any stock — only basic balance sheet and earnings statistics, which I call the skeleton. However, a person — or a corporation — is far more than a skeleton. A skeleton is not alive, but most companies are very much so. They are beehives of activity.

What I do have is knowledge of whether a market is cheap or expensive. This knowledge is based on historical data such as the price/earnings ratio (how many times the annual profit you pay when you buy a stock) and the market's average dividend yield. If markets are priced way below average valuation, I conclude the market is cheap and vice versa. Today's stock markets are expensive by many of these yardsticks. But I do not buy the stock market, only individual stocks. Still, when markets are cheap there are more cheap stocks than when they are high!

I also know a few other general aspects of stock prices. For instance, when interest rates are high, stocks tend to be cheaper than when they are low. Oddly, mostly when inflation is high, high interest rates make for low stock prices, just when logic tells you that stocks, not money values, will survive the inflation. So 1980 and 1981 were great times to buy stocks, as were the early 1970s, when explosive inflation followed the skyrocketing of oil prices upon the rise to prominence of the OPEC cartel. These kinds of guideposts have proven quite helpful.

The imperative, therefore, is to have an investment policy that performs better but involves less risk than the markets overall. There are a number of policies that over years have been successful when practised in a disciplined and informed manner.

Index funds are a really good low-cost investment tool. Assume we start with the S&P/TSX Composite Index or, in the US, the S&P 500 index. The makeup of these indexes doesn't change much, apart from the occasional replacement of certain stocks with others that are performing better. So index funds, on the whole, do little trading and do not pay commissions. Therefore, unless you can make trades that earn you more money than the commission cost, the index fund is a better bet.

However, buying an index fund won't enable you to meet your long-term objective of outperforming the market. In contrast, if you act on your own, you have the advantage of not riding stocks up or down, as an index does. For instance, if an average price/earnings ratio has historically been 14 to 15 times earnings and it goes up to 24 to 26 times, as has recently been the case, you can reduce the number of stocks you own in favour of cash or short-term bonds. In 1972, you could have added to your portfolio at an average price/earnings ratio of under 10 times. You can fine-tune even more than that, and, if you have a good reading on individual shares, you can buy or sell accordingly as they get undervalued and overvalued.

Looking at an index, it is clear that some industries are very mature and will never bring more than below-average returns, while others will do better. Historically, raw material or commodity prices have not kept up with inflation; whereas other sectors, such as health care or finance, have exceeded it. Apart from that, an index inevitably includes a few companies that are badly managed, as well as some smaller doubtful enterprises that have a perennially low rate of return — or are outright money losers.

In this manner you might eliminate a minimum of 60% of the S&P 500 index. Whenever a group is swept suddenly into fashion you can reduce or eliminate your holding of those stocks for a while, and similarly, when a good group or company is unpopular or has fallen in the short-term only, you can add them to your portfolio. Companies with excessive debt in normal or recessive times should be avoided altogether. It is best also to bypass possible bankruptcies. This approach should, again, enable you to whittle down the undesirable names quite materially.

Then look at the remaining companies. How many are cyclical? Will you be able to correctly judge cyclical tops and get out in time, so you won't have to wait for the next top five years later? Or would it be easier to eliminate all cyclicals except those that can be purchased when they are at the bottom (if, that is, you are sure the company will survive)? If you can buy at the bottom, you can then get an easy double and sell them well below the top, thus avoiding the risk that the price will skid back down before you sell. This can be a tricky game, however, and the question is, is it more rewarding in the long term to just stick with non-cyclical, quality growth stocks? My preference is for the latter — it is easier to sleep, there are fewer transactions, and you avoid the annoyance of buying too early or missing the sale near the top. Also, non-cyclical growth stocks periodically raise dividends, while cyclicals raise and lower them.

Once when I was young, I drove a very old car from Holland to France. My uncle in the Netherlands advised that all the long stretches be done on the major highways rather than along the scenic side roads. The reason? There is less chance of accidents, you get there faster, and if the car breaks down you can get help quickly. It's good advice for investments too: Stay with the big non-cyclicals on the long-term highway of investment.

Out of the many thousands of stocks I can choose from worldwide, I therefore really only need look at 50 at most. I need not buy BCE or General Motors if I don't think that these companies can consistently generate earnings for many years ahead at 14 to 16% annually. And the same thing goes for paper company stocks, since the industry is predominantly cyclical and commodity returns rarely allow 14 to 16% long-term growth. I also need not buy small junior stocks that could be killed by some competitor entering and overnight ruining the profit margins, or worse.

I also do not believe in buying companies that do not pay attractive dividends — preferably rising dividends with rising company fortunes! Corporations, like most living organisms, have a life span. A corporation is for profit and this profit accrues to the shareholder. But it is possible for a corporation to go from birth to death without giving the total sum of shareholders anything. Some investors might trade the shares and reap a profit, but in time, as the company declines, others would lose, and the initial investment would be totally wiped out if the company or its successors went bust.

So to me dividends are important. Management, workers, the banks, the tax collectors, the community — everyone gets paid, even the board of directors. So why not also the shareholder? Dividends should rise as fast as the salary mass of the executive group — or, in fact, faster, since it is the shareholders who take all the financial risk!

Nobody can forecast the future. But it's obvious that companies that have a strong, uninterrupted record are more interesting than those that have not. There is no certainty, of course, that the trend will continue. There is no certainty, ever, in the stock market. However, if you have access to a company's competitors, especially someone well-informed, you can get an excellent reading on the company's management, strategy, and products. And for many consumer companies you can even get this in the marketplace. Retailers — or even simply your friends and acquaintances — probably have opinions on the quality of most consumer products; your doctor or your druggist sees how efficacious drugs are or how well they sell. And as mentioned before, many of the companies you want to own shares in are, in fact, makers of non-cyclical consumer products.

The consumption of peanut butter, cereals, soft drinks, or razor blades is essentially non-cyclical. Moreover, with the end of the Cold War and the demise of Communism, these products have invaded the entire globe. The leading companies have the benefit of lower per unit production costs and so can amass larger profits, thus providing more cash to push their expansions. Their marketing networks are very strong and can be used to promote newly developed products or those acquired through takeovers. Being the leaders, their larger profit margins permit both growth and dividends, while the number two or three companies may well have to choose between one or the other.

Thus companies like Gillette, Coca-Cola, Philip Morris, Unilever, Kellogg, ConAgra, etc., are the types of firms worth considering. You should examine the growth rate of their earnings and dividends over a period of, say, 10 years. If they doubled every five to seven years, you are looking at candidates for your investment program. If, moreover, the share price has gone up four times in 10 years without the price/earnings ratio expanding, you are looking at the kind of stock you should have bought 10 years ago!

There are many ways to check how the company you are looking at is viewed by knowledgeable analysts. Firstly, you can simply read the newspapers, since many evaluations are published. Secondly, you can talk to analysts at financial firms, explain your investment policy, and ask them to suggest candidates for your portfolio. The Internet can also be a source of information and ideas. And, if you have access to Bloomberg or similar research services, you could run a "screen" to find stocks that meet your criterion of earnings growth at 14% or more on a stable progression.

Look at stocks from all over the world; but if you buy foreign stocks, try to confine yourself to those listed in New York, as this assures that accounting and listing requirements are valid. Many countries have little regulation and, consequently, little shareholder protection. Many of the leading European, South American, and Asian companies you may want to look at have so-called American Depository Receipts, which provide protection. Most of the desirable companies you will find, however, are US companies.

Another very fertile area for your search is health care, including the leading hospital supply stocks. These include companies such as Abbott Laboratories, Johnson & Johnson, Novartis (a Swiss company), Hoffmann-La Roche (also Swiss), Cardinal Health, Pfizer, Amgen, etc. These are all major concerns with strong franchises and outstanding research facilities. To my mind this is a marvellous area and I have always held large positions in these industries in my portfolios.

Retail and distribution also will yield some good stocks, but this is a trickier area. The leading drugstore chains, for instance, have terrific proven records. But a retail concept often has a limited life span that can be difficult to extend. The top food chains prove more likely to perpetuate themselves than department stores or speciality outfits. Still, if you catch a good concept early, like a Wal-Mart or Home Depot, it may provide you with 15% growth for a good number of years.

It is hard to find 15% stable growth in the banking or insurance fields, but it does exist, particularly recently. Changes in competition laws have blurred the lines between underwriting, brokerage, insurance, and banking, creating new opportunities for development. The consequence is a worldwide service expansion. There are many stocks in this sector that provide solid returns of around 12 to 13% annually. Of course, you should watch interest rates, because higher rates tend to dampen the share prices of these stocks. Look for financial stocks that have a high return on shareholders' equity year in and year out and a growing revenue line, showing that there is solid growth both on top (gross income) and at the bottom (net income). Again, by and large, look for leaders. Size, provided it is well-managed, provides lower unit costs and a competitive advantage, and this accounts for the current strong merger trend.

I recommend a measure of industry diversification, but it need not be excessive. There is no reason not to have 20% or so of your investments in any major group, so that four or five broad categories, plus some speciality areas, such as entertainment, communications, and electrical equipment, could round out your portfolio.

What you want to avoid is getting sucked into industries that do not match the profile discussed above. In high-tech there are many, many firms that can do very well over a number of years, but then collapse, as did Apple, Wang Labs, Unisys, and Digital, to name a few. The emphasis in these cases is not so much on the products they have today as on whether they have access to the best innovative young people coming out of graduate or engineering school. The success of Microsoft or Cisco lies in this area, just as it did at certain times for Intel, Nortel, or Ericsson. You can sample the best of these, but once again stay on the highway, and don't be seduced onto the byway, however scenic the latter may look to you.

The crux of your success will be selecting leading companies' stocks and then holding on to them for many years. While you cannot go to sleep, and there is a place for monitoring, there is no reason to panic if a firm has earnings that fall short in a given year or two. This is quite a normal phenomenon. Companies, unless they "manage their earnings" (short for trying to manipulate them), inevitably go through periods that are better or worse. Most companies, even the very best, must continually reinvent themselves. In many firms, products that have come out in the previous three to four years may represent 40 to 50% of total sales. And in the pharmaceutical industry, drugs go off patent and then face competition from the so-called generics. So if the pipeline has nothing spectacularly new, there will be a slowdown, a lull. This need not be worrisome if research quality and overall management remain "top-flight." I once purchased stock in Pfizer (a major pharmaceutical company) in one of these lulls, only to see it quadruple in the following four years.

This investment approach makes for relatively dull investing, as there are normally few surprises and not much day-to-day movement. But it works, especially if you add expert research. Stay disciplined and stay on the main highway — don't look all around. You are not seeking an emotional fix — unlike at the casino, you don't invest for the entertainment value but rather to make safe and sound money in the long term.

Chapter 8

A Tale
of Three Stocks

You really only need to know the basics to get a solid start in stock market investing. Of course there will be the inevitable mistakes. Even I make them. (If I was perfect I wouldn't run an investment counsel firm; I could sit on the beach and make a few single $1 billion decisions every few years!) What is important is not avoiding mistakes entirely, but being able to see your mistakes and make fewer as time goes by. You should not be repeating your mistakes — especially the obvious ones. Above all, stick with your policies.

Even the world renowned investor Warren Buffett has never hesitated to acknowledge his mistakes. He has shown himself to be a master at benefiting from the compounding of values over time by buying the very best non-cyclical consumer growth stocks and holding on to them over long periods. He has paid close attention to the quality of management in the companies he invests in, and, when it has failed to live up to expectations, he has taken action. He bought Coca-Cola and Gillette and saw their value double in five years, a rate he continues to achieve with these stocks. He has, on the other hand, sold securities when his initial judgment was proved wrong — in the case of

USAir, for instance. But in all cases, he only sold when he was certain the company's underperformance reflected not a temporary setback but a permanent problem.

You should diversify your holdings, but you should only diversify among the very best. Of course, if you are able to buy stock when its price is experiencing a major, but temporary, dip, your compounding forward will be faster — and vice versa. At present there are few low-priced stocks, but if a stock's earnings can continue to accelerate at 20% per year, you could afford to pay a bit more per share to get in, buying more if the prices drop.

Say you start with $200 000. To diversify you should have some 20 stocks, each at a cost of maybe $10 000. As long as you have made rational choices you need sell neither the winners nor the losers. If you know (through a process of reasoning, not through fear because the stock is down) your choice was wrong, then correct your mistake early on by selling the stock. Other than that, let time and compound growth do their work.

Clearly your choice of investments determines the result. Some 50 years ago I invested $2000 each in three very different stocks. The first was Reynolds Metals, a producer of aluminum, the fastest growing major metal of its day. I held those shares, finally selling them in 2000 when Reynolds was merged with rival Alcoa, at which point they were worth $15 000. As you know, 50 years ago a Coke or cup of coffee cost 5 cents, so there is no need to tell you that this was a rather poor investment. I could possibly have earned a bit more had I sold Reynolds, repurchased, and sold it a few times. Each time, though, I would have had to pay capital gains tax on the profit and may well have ended up with little more. So despite its "wonder metal" outlook in 1948, Reynolds Metals turned out to be a poor investment.

The second share I bought was United Airlines (UAL). It too looked like a terrific bet. The commercial airline industry was still in its infancy. The jet engine had just made its appearance and the belief was that the whole world would soon be flying — and so it was. The industry grew by leaps and bounds, and UAL became, for a time, the world's largest airline. Not a bad bet, right? Maybe not. Airlines over-expanded. In order to service huge debts, they had to fill their planes, and the resulting competition for passengers drove ticket prices down — thereby driving profits to the vanishing point. Many airlines went to the wall, and for many years UAL had losses and could not pay dividends. Then suddenly, some 15 years ago, airlines became market darlings. On a takeover offer (which in time collapsed) UAL stock, which I had bought at $12 per share, rose to $284 per share (35 years after purchase), as the takeover was planned to take place around $300. I sold the shares at $282, after which the stock collapsed to $80 again. Did I make big money? Well, I had to pay a huge capital gains tax, and remember that Coke and coffee had each cost 5 cents in 1948!

The third stock was less flamboyant than aluminum or air travel, and seemed far less exciting when I bought it. It was Abbott Laboratories. Abbott had few ups and downs over the years, gradually growing by 10 to 16% annually in earnings and dividends. Very seldom was the stock spectacular either way. It took a big dip once when its intravenous products were discovered to be contaminated. But, by and large, it offered a steady 10 to 16% compound growth. Dividends rose almost every year in the 50-year period. The $2 000 today, not including dividends, has grown to some $1 million. There was never a good reason to sell, only to buy more — unlike UAL or Reynolds Metals. So the taxman will have to wait a bit longer, apart from the tax on dividends!

Which stock gave me the least stress and the soundest sleep? Abbott Laboratories, of course. Which entailed the least risk? Abbott. So do you have to take great risks to reap big profits? Obviously not in this case. And, I maintain, perhaps not in any case. All through the years, the risk or volatility factor of Abbott Laboratories was lower than that of either UAL or Reynolds Metals. Compound growth worked for Abbott. It did not provide much in the other two cases.

Making money in stocks without heeding the laws of compound growth is inevitably very expensive — or a question of just plain luck. Luck exists in every life, of course. But most people don't recognize the lady even when she flaunts herself! In the case of Abbott Laboratories, however, it was not luck — rather it was patience and keeping an eye on certain fundamentals. There were many years when UAL or Reynolds Metals rose a higher percentage than Abbott. Not that Abbott was a tortoise in a race with hares! On the contrary, Abbott was a steady winner. Unlike the other two, it was largely non-cyclical, and its rate of compounding could be closely monitored. Its growth was at a rate that provided a double in most five- to seven-year periods. In fact, had it averaged more, it might in time have attracted greater competition.

Abbott was well-managed and gradually gained on its competition. It had a solid stream of new products, a good research effort, and a fine sales organization. It was the kind of stock that provided predictable compound growth at an optimum rate. How many Abbotts do you need to assure your retirement if you start at age 20? Very few! There is room to make mistakes. However, I certainly learned a very important lesson over the past 50 years: Look for Abbotts and stay away from Reynolds Metals and UALs! At one time, stocks like Abbott received the name of "one decision stock." In the 1960s, they were also known as the "Nifty Fifty." At that time, though, they became vastly overpriced in terms of their then current earnings.

However, even based on those high prices, 25 to 30 years later their returns have been excellent. Would it have made much difference had I paid $4000 or $6000 instead of $2000 in 1948? I tell the story of Jesus, whose father gave him $100 at birth and in his omniscience and omnipotence assured him that the money would double every five years. Between 1999 and 2004, Jesus' investment grew as much in dollars as it did in the first 1999 years! The trick is in compounding at the highest rate possible — but at low risk, of course. That way, your possibilities for gain just keep on multiplying.

Taxes also play a role. Capital gains taxes in Canada on long-term holdings are one half of the income tax rates. However, taxation does not make any allowance for inflation. Say you bought a stock at $20 two decades ago and the dollar only buys 25 cents of what it purchased then. If the stock now sells at $80, you actually have no profit in real terms whatsoever. (Before capital gains tax, the value of your stock — in terms of its purchasing power after inflation — is exactly what it was when you bought the stock.) And if you sold the stock, you might pay — as you would in Quebec, for instance — some 25% of the $60 "profit." This is $15 per share. You now have only $65 of current money left — and because of inflation you have actually lost $15 (in terms of purchasing power) over the 20 years you held the stock. So the capital gains tax was well over 100% of the gain. So it is important to choose stocks that will provide the best return after inflation and taxes.

You should also aim for stocks with little dependence on business cycles. In that way, you will not have to sell them early, they will continue to bear fruit — and only when you sell them much later will the government profit! In the case of a non-taxable investment account such as a Registered Retirement Savings Plan (RRSP) or other pension plan, you can buy cyclicals. But since they entail more risk (as you can overstay a cycle and have to wait four years for the next one), make sure that you get out close to the cycle peaks. There is little sense in assuming more risk to get less reward. Personally, I only invest in cyclicals by exception and only if I can buy them really cheap at market bottoms. I always get out "too early" thus leaving something on the table, since getting out too late is an absolute "no-no!"

If you have premium high compound growth non-cyclicals, it is not really necessary to get out if the stock price goes high. If far too high, obviously you can trim a bit and pay some tax, but be sure that your gains have been real, not inflation mirages. Personally, I normally just hold and take a few down drafts, counting on the next bull market to take me up again. Don't forget that if your company's earnings grow at 15 or 20%, an overvaluation of that order will be made up in one year. In contrast, the tax you pay on a sale is gone forever, leaving you with up to 25% less money than what you were getting from dividends before your sale. Even if your cost was next to nil, as in my Abbott Laboratories example, $100 of so-called "profit" may shrink to as low as $60 after tax, which means that the stock has to drop 40% before you can buy back the same quantity. With a good stock in a taxable account, it is much easier just to stick with it.

Chapter 9

An Investor,
Not a Gambler Be

As I said in previous chapters, I believe that you buy individual stocks and not the whole market. And while I urge you to always put an emphasis on quality, you should not neglect quantity either.

Here is what I mean: Coca-Cola is a quality stock. Standard & Poor's rates it A+, its highest rating. Assuming earnings of $1 per share, you will agree that it is obviously better to buy Coca-Cola at $15 per share rather than at $45. This way, you can buy three times as many shares for the same amount of money. So even if you are a long-term investor (planning to hold the stock for, say, 25 years), the best time to buy or to add to your holding of a quality stock is still when the share price is low.

Following the same logic, you might want to sell your Coca-Cola shares today, while the price is high, hoping for a cheaper price later on. If you are non-taxable this is not unrealistic and, while it would not be a good idea to lose your whole position, you might do it with part. Forget about the adage, "You never lose money taking a profit," because over the past 40 years anyone who sold Coca-Cola and didn't repurchase cheaper later has regretted it (and few did repurchase; far more simply regret their decision to sell).

I try to maximize the quantity of shares I can buy by looking for low valuations. Clearly this optimizes the compound growth potential. If you buy shares cheap and then they go up to an average valuation, you have gotten a "free ride" on that increase in value. Conversely, your rate of return is reduced if you buy an overpriced share and in time the stock returns to an average or below-average valuation.

There are many policies such as this which, if well practised, can provide you with good medium- or long-term market results. Personally, I am risk-averse, so I want all my stocks to be of high quality. I will not confuse you with other policies that lead to more volatile results. Over the years, I have tried many of them, but I found that, psychologically, I was just not comfortable with them.

Other than once early in my career, I have never sold a stock "short," that is, sold something I did not own, hoping to buy it back at a lower price. I have never been a "momentum" investor, that is, buying a stock with a strong upward price curve hoping that I can get out before it reverses. I have never purchased shares of companies whose products I do not understand. I have never bought stock of companies when I felt that I could not judge how competitive the company would remain in a year or two. I have not purchased shares of companies in industries where I was not fairly sure that new innovation could not knock them out. Thus high-tech — apart from the very, very strongest companies in market position and management ability — I have always counted too risky for me.

Management quality plays a major role in your stock picking process. We have seen top companies (General Motors, AT&T, U.S. Steel, etc.) decline as the result of poor top management. Sometimes it is a question of "resting on one's laurels." Other times, it is foolish acquisitions or overexpansion. There are a myriad reasons. The culture of a company is very important. Does it attract and keep the very best people? Procter & Gamble has always been a very strong company, despite the fact that it has lost many brilliant people to competitors. Their policy of hiring the best people out of school gave them an overabundance of good people, many of whom have gone on to superb careers elsewhere. P&G became a school for quality young executives.

But how do you check on management quality? The simplest way by far is to ask the competition. If you don't have access to these people yourself, most analysts that do field trip work have asked these questions: Who is the toughest competitor? Which company do people admire the most? The answers will give you a pretty good idea of which companies have high quality management. At a bank board meeting in Switzerland, I asked a very old, clever director what he considered the most important thing for a director to watch. His answer was quite clear: "Do we have the best management in the industry? Will we have the best management in the industry?"

When there is good management, a director's task is easy. Things get done right, and at board meetings, management is capable of intelligently answering any and all questions. Such managers will regard board members as mentors, not police. They will not fear questions or comments, but rather welcome them. Good management, of course, has a side that is hard to define. It is more than just brain power and knowing what should be done and how to do it efficiently. It also involves people skills — the ability to build an organization with a culture of dynamism and enthusiasm that can drive it forward. Clearly, these skills are not "a dime a dozen." And finding them makes all the difference. If a company doesn't have them, watch out!

The people who manage companies are no different from other human beings. They have the same emotional hang-ups. Some executives are smart, rational, and careful — but not all of them. Some enjoy taking ego trips with other people's money. Some are diffident — incapable of making tough decisions and incapable of firing people, but infighters when someone threatens their job. Some like the position because they are attracted to the soft life that can go with it: planes, yachts, houses, golf clubs, you name it. But these personal shortcomings detract from the ability to actually manage well — to make the activities and the problems of the company one's first priority day after day, night and day.

From the investor's point of view, what it boils down to is that well-managed companies have a far better chance of success than poorly managed ones, and the latter, despite fine assets, are to be avoided unless you can buy them out and install good managers who are truly committed to the company: "24-7 people."

A friend of mine has built a $4 billion mega-fortune on just this principle — buying badly managed assets and turfing out everyone who wasn't suitable. His main achievement has been finding good people and helping them perform well.

Knowing the people who manage a company is, therefore, all-important. There are builders; there are looters; there are good and poor managers. Some are ultra-conservative; others roll the dice. Managers of small companies almost form a category of their own. In a small company, it is possible for top executive's salaries to take up too great a percentage of revenue or gross margins. And a scandal in a small company is rarely reported to the world at large. It is an advantage to the investor that large companies are much more in the spotlight and, until recently, salaries and other executive remuneration were mostly kept within reasonable bounds.

Apart from the senior managers, it is important to watch majority shareholders, especially those who draw recompense from the company. And the composition of boards is of interest as well: Cronies and "yes-men" offer little protection to minority shareholders. I cannot emphasize enough that the competence and integrity of the people who manage your companies is crucial in your choice of stocks.

At times I do dabble with smaller, though largely non-cyclical, stocks. But I have never put a large percentage of my resources in these, and they still have to meet some basic conditions: Their area of business is one that I understand, they are stable enough to attract and keep good people, they conform with sound accounting principles, and they have managers who are disciplined and competent with strong ethics — and their feet on the ground. I like companies that do things extremely well, regardless of the seductions of sweet-talking investment bankers. A small company with managers and staff who work extremely hard — with intelligence and integrity and a strong customer focus — will have no trouble outdistancing the competition. Buying stock in such companies really is no more than adding more junior non-cyclicals to your portfolio, hoping that they will eventually grow to match your normal portfolio profile.

I have friends in the investment management business who have specialized in small companies — their stock in trade being trying to identify good management at a very early stage. Some have been extremely successful in the long term, but short-term value swings can be huge, even if you diversify over 40 or 50 stocks. This kind of investing takes extreme alertness and an intimate knowledge of the people who control and run the companies. You also have to limit what percentage of the company you own, in order to limit the damage should something go wrong.

Small companies generate very little trading – sometimes none at all. But a very little stock volume can push these shares up or down by huge percentages. It is a style of investment management that I understand, but which I don't really like because it does not allow me to develop very large pools of stock to manage. Jarislowsky Fraser has tried this approach a few times, but with less than stellar results. In the course of our history, this kind of investment might have absorbed, at times, up to 10% of our equity positions.

It's not enough for a company to have good management just for today. It also must be working to ensure it will have good management tomorrow. Unless a company is demoralized (like IBM some years ago), an outsider will have difficulty being accepted into the company culture. So normally it must try to develop tomorrow's managers from within the organization. Again this strategy centres on consistently hiring the best young people that can be found and then providing them with a climate in which they can grow and enjoy their work. Today's world is increasingly for the young, and the best innovative, creative work is and has always been done by people between 17 and 40 years of age, as these people explore their identities, strengths, and limitations. Having a young, competent team is especially essential in new services and high-tech, where so much explosive growth is taking place today.

Another factor to keep your eye on is the level of debt in a company. Many distinguished firms have been wrecked by over-ambitious expansion or megalomania, expressed through excessive acquisition activity at too high a price. Investment bankers alternatively encourage mergers (with high fees payable to them) and, later, divestiture (also with high fees payable to them). Most acquisitions do not work out, as there are often huge cultural differences within the companies and the sellers usually lose interest once they have big sums of money in their pockets. And pride and competitiveness often induce a company to pay too much. The graveyards of companies that shouldered excessive debt are extensive. "Pride goes before a fall," is the saying. Executive pride and vanity should not be underestimated.

Remember you are looking for low-risk, high compound interest investment over time. You are not looking for a "killing"; you are not a gambler. So gamble as little as possible — while always acknowledging that any investment involves some risk.

Chapter 10

A Sound,
"Do-It-Yourself" Approach

The beauty of the high-quality, worldwide, non-cyclical approach is that it gives a good reward while being low-risk, simple, non-commission intensive, and exposed to few surprises. I have often recommended it to people who want to build a simple, sound portfolio and do not have the capital to go to investment counsel. It adapts well to a do-it-yourself approach, because there is no need for constant, high-quality security analysis to support it — which a management firm can provide, but often at a hefty price.

First of all, don't complicate things with a lot of variables that you will have to keep track of. Keep it simple. Avoid frequent trading, develop long-term rather than short-term policies, don't try to guess the length of cycles, and forget strategies that require a lot of knowledge or constant research. And don't get led astray. There are siren songs all around you: All kinds of intermediaries will want you to part with your money. Don't be sold, be a buyer. The game I suggest is not very complicated and it works. "You can paddle your own canoe" with great confidence.

As your fortune expands, it will become easier to hire professional advice — although by that time you may well have become quite a skilful semi-professional yourself. So why pay for what you are already good at? What a professional organization of quality can provide is the research team to find and monitor stocks that fit your investment criteria. You might also be able to find an experienced, wealthy-in-his-own-right broker who follows a similar philosophy with his own investments and who has a vast research group at his beck and call. Use whatever advice and research are available, but remain a buyer. Don't be sold on something a salesperson is offering! Another resource can be other investors like yourself, and discussions with them can be extremely fruitful.

One thing I always warn against is excessive information and getting bogged down in excessive detail. Information and details change and a year later are stale and of little use. Turn over the major stones for sure — do your homework well. But keep the woods in view, and don't get lost in the trees. You are trying to pick stocks you can be married to for many, many years for the most part. Any piece of news may create great excitement for a few weeks or months, but it may have little significance three or five years from now. The main things to look for are: 1) a fast growing, non-cyclical industry; 2) the best company in it; and 3) the assurance of excellent management both today and in the future. If there is more than one best company, buy both!

While I said in an earlier chapter that if all goes well (which it never does!) $10 000 can become $2.5 million in 40 years, I'm not suggesting that you should stop investing new money after the first $10 000. On the contrary, I suggest you make room in your annual budget for a very specific sum of savings. As stock prices fluctuate, this money can be kept in short-term paper until one or more of your favourite stocks becomes available at a low valuation, which inevitably happens from time to time.

For example, Philip Morris shares may slump because of worry about tobacco lawsuits. But this will undoubtedly be temporary. Tobacco demand is inelastic, which means that if people want to smoke they will do so at any price. So the cost of the lawsuits will probably only mean a higher retail price to offset it, which will ultimately have little impact on the company's bottom line.

The US government may make noises about regulating pharmaceutical prices, and Pfizer shares may drop as a result. But Pfizer sells all over the world to a population much bigger than that of the United States. So load up on it or any other top-notch health care stocks before the dust settles. Some of the shrewdest investors buy top-quality stocks when things are in temporary disarray as a matter of policy.

Buying is obviously easier than selling. It is relatively easy to spot a good stock and to buy it. But capital gains tax, as we have seen, is an impediment to intelligent investing. Due to inflation, it is effectively probably the highest tax in the land, especially in a country like Canada. There are two reasons to sell: 1) the stock has gone much too high; and 2) the company no longer fits the criteria of your investment policy — that is, it is no longer at and will probably not in the future return to your minimum rate of compound growth; it has taken on too much debt; or it is losing its position and is poorly managed.

I always ask myself the question: Would I buy the stock today? If not, you should ask yourself whether you should hold it. I don't mean that the stock is fully priced and that I would prefer to buy at a bargain level. Rather, is it of the quality, does it still have the characteristics that match my investment policy? Is it a name that fully fits my guidelines? If it is, I keep it. If not, I look closely at its prospects and at alternatives. Since I am essentially a long-term investor, I do not make decisions lightly or quickly. It is not a matter of just making a "smart switch," as my favourite broker would suggest. Patience is an integral quality of a great investor.

If you need to sell, get rid of any cyclical stocks, low-quality issues, or gambling shares — all those animals from the zoo that you don't want. Even if you may on occasion bitterly regret it, clear these noxious pests right out. Above all, make sure you pursue your investment policy religiously with your main funds.

Use high markets to get rid of weak companies and investment mistakes. Hold the cash so that you can buy the quality ones when the down draft comes. Investors who did this in the past got an enormous return a few years later when they could use that cash to buy at half the peak price or less. Always keep a list of top-quality stocks that you would buy in the next major slump.

But the markets still haven't dipped far enough for that yet. And, in 2005, because of the weakening of the American dollar, Canadian currency stocks became more interesting: Their profit outside the US when translated into American dollars increases considerably. Interest rates will not rise significantly for a while and so sound income stocks (dividend payers) should be held. As well, top-notch quality, non-cyclical shares, such as drugstore chains and medical equipment stocks, will continue to have good results. Soft drinks, beer, tobacco, liquor, and brand foods should hold up reasonably well and grow with population increases. Low interest rates will sustain their price/earnings ratios. If I am right, it is too late to buy cyclicals, secondary companies, or gambling stocks, not to mention high-tech or related issues. Also remember there are very few if any "safe" stocks left. Deregulation and worldwide competition have ended that period. So it is essential to diversify even among leading, well-managed non-cyclicals.

If good investing is essentially as rational as possible a pursuit and stock prices fluctuate around rational levels in normal times, then the "panics and bubbles" that appear from time to time in the markets present especially good opportunities to buy or sell. Panics normally drop stocks faster than bubbles lift them. And panics are most rapid initially and then subside, while bubbles tend to feed on themselves and gather momentum.

If, say, 14 times earnings represents an average market, then don't get sucked into accepting 20 or 25 times as normal, even though shares may maintain such a level for extended periods; this is simply a bubble. Similarly, in a bear market, an average 8 to 12 times multiple, even if maintained over long periods — especially after a major panic or in a deep recession — is probably still worth buying. If in the long term stocks yield 5 to 6% after inflation, then buying at an above-average market level will yield less — while the converse is equally true.

Panics, once you examine the reasons for them, are rarely justified. But panic, by definition, is irrational. The one following the September 11, 2001 attack on New York was necessarily short-term. There was no repetition of the event that triggered it, and as a result the fear could not be sustained (though caution was). On the other hand, the panic of June–July 2002 was far more dangerous and destructive of long-term value. That one was precipitated by massive mutual fund redemptions and a simultaneous selling of the US dollar by foreigners, following a rash of corporate scandals and executive looting sprees. Pension fund restructuring away from equities to more predictable bonds was also a contributor. At the same time, the general illusion of wealth, collapsing under the weight of excessive consumer and corporate debt, gave way to the prospect of a lengthy recession, sending investors fleeing.

Once mutual fund owners run for cash, the funds must sell forthwith. And if the bids are scarce, they will do so at ever-lower prices, irrespective of long-term value or quality. This affects the best stocks that have large public floats above all, as they are among the few that are easy to sell, due to high marketability (liquidity). So a panic among unsophisticated mutual fund owners can wreak havoc that lasts for quite a while — until the shares are finally in strong hands only — and for mutual funds there are precious few of those. Not many of these shares were actively, intelligently purchased in the first place; mostly they were bought when the mutual fund concept was enjoying a phase of popularity and gains were easy to come by.

In a short-term panic (such as that following 9/11), you can buy almost immediately. In the case of a longer-term crisis (such as June–July 2002), take your time. Allow at least six months to pass. After that, the panic will subside and a new era will begin. "Don't stand in front of a freight train," as the saying goes. There will be lots of time! Admittedly, you will get cheap stocks quite early, but don't "buy cheap to sell cheaper!" Just wait until the panic has exhausted itself fully and the recession is at a very deep point. Then, when "all is darkness," you will have your pick, and your patience will be well rewarded. I have another saying. If you want to buy cheap from scared people: "Why jump on a moving freight train and rob it if you can just wait until it stops?"

Panic is a short-term emotion. And as such an investor should not give way to it. Rather, he might benefit from it by following my rule of being a "gentleman." When Nortel reached $120 and demand for the shares was unlimited, a true gentleman owning shares would have sold them to be kind to the buyers. Similarly, when it got to $3, I was nice to the desperate sellers and obliged them by taking shares off their hands. Panics exaggerate things in the short term. Most panics are "sell" ones; buying panics exist but are rare, so do not worry too much about them. The latter are usually confined to certain groups such as dot coms, high-techs, or the "new economy." So since panics do not last, provided the market was already at relatively depressed levels (but not if stocks were overvalued), they represent superb buying opportunities. On Monday, September 17, 2001, I placed a number of buying orders into the market on stocks that I felt were high quality and had already been reasonably priced. I did not get all my orders filled, but I was a gentleman on some.

Investment management must always balance facts, logic, and common sense against temporary emotion or prejudices. Once you learn this, you look at down panics as opportunities — not as something to get depressed about. Similarly, if there is an "up panic," you try to curb your greed and refrain from joining in the fray; let others have their short-term fun. To hold firm to your investment policies when you have "mouth-watering" cheap stocks all around takes discipline, but discipline is possibly the most important tool of the investor.

Stock markets for many people are an emotional outlet. Every day provides a thrill of pain or pleasure. Many people have trouble blocking this out — and many do not even want to. For many elderly people, watching the stock market is a full working day activity, compensating for the fact that most of their real emotional life now resides in the distant past.

Panics are far more stressful than bubble markets. Instead of arousing the acquisitive instincts as bubbles do, panics, for many, seem to spell total disaster: "The sky is falling! Better save what I can, albeit at the price of a huge loss." But both can cause stress. And the stakes are higher for elderly people than they are for the young. There is no time left to recoup, and what jobs are there for 70-year-olds? So, apart from the very wealthy, older people should probably largely own bonds. But "one man's meat is another man's poison" and for the rational, disciplined investor with good knowledge, panics and bubbles do not need to be a source of stress and agony; they are instead rare opportunities.

Chapter 11

Looking Beyond the Skeleton

Good security analysis is essential to a strong, rational investment approach, since buying and selling should be based on the best information. Such information should be at the heart of a solid investment approach, which aims to outperform the markets at a lower level of risk than the market itself.

As a young security analyst in the mid- and late-1950s, I taught a course in the graduate program of the McGill University School of Commerce. I used Graham and Dodd's *Security Analysis* as the main text. But I also asked each student to read 150 pages of stock market biographies and history to supplement the more technical problem solving. It takes competence plus *experience* to be a successful security analyst and the latter texts provided some of that.

Security analysis is far more than technical competence. That is a bit like the skeleton of a beautiful woman — it misses the essence. Yet, more often than not, security analysts concentrate most of their effort on income ratios, adjusted past earnings, and balance sheet analysis to pronounce value. The future is normally extrapolated at assumed growth rates. Unfortunately, while this gives you 20/20 hindsight, it does not really approximate a future never fully predictable and usually full of surprises.

This is not to say that statistical analysis is not valuable. Balance sheet solidity is one of the first things I look at when studying a stock. For instance, an over-indebted company often indicates a management with overblown egos, and that eventually spells trouble. Over the long run, making big money is difficult unless there is strong growth, and this cannot be reliably achieved if there is excessive debt. Although it is possible for a company to succeed in spite of having some bad years, excessive debt means living with a sword of Damocles over your head. I find it easier to live without one. Bad luck is unavoidable at times. So why go looking for it?

Analysis requires you to look at debt carefully. One hundred million dollars of debt is not always just that. If it is all due next year, it is far more dangerous than if repayments are spread out over many future years. If it has an 8% coupon, it is very different from debt with a 4% coupon. However, if it is in a foreign currency that normally is stronger than yours, 4% can take on a far more dangerous meaning. If it is bank debt (short-term), part of current liabilities, you must remember that a bank is your friend only in good times. Never trust a bank when you're in need. Banks hate loans then and will do all they can to avoid loan default. They can turn on a dime if they begin to feel that the loan may have to be downgraded or written off as a "bad debt." To understand this, put yourself in the shoes of a banker[1].

So let me review some of the key metrics I look at when evaluating a company.

---

[1]   Any intelligent lender would do the same. A money manager, like myself, will sell a bond at the least sign of trouble ahead. I buy a bond because I believe it is totally safe; all I'm interested in is getting maximum interest with total safety. You never make up in additional interest what you would lose in a default. When a bond becomes unsafe, I normally sell it as fast as possible and replace it with a safe one.

Bank debt normally should not exceed accounts receivable. Accounts receivable are self-liquidating and so assure the corporation that bank debt is no long-term danger — no danger at all, in fact — unless there is a major spike in interest rates. In that case, if it can, the company should increase its margin of profit to offset the higher debt cost. Long-term assets, such as plant equipment, should not be financed with short-term debt.

If a company has long-term debt on which interest and debt repayment must be met, then it is important to have cash income (net income plus depreciation) before tax that easily covers the interest demands at all times. If it does, repayments — if the need arises — can be refinanced. If not, the company had better build up sufficient liquidity not to run into a temporary, possibly fatal, problem.

So margins of profit and cash income stream are important for debt management. These also are important for growth, as the reason you own a stock in the long term is earnings and cash income growth. If earnings do not grow over the years, then all your stock will do is bob up and down, based on perceived short-term fortunes or changes in interest rates and shareholder expectations. You can make or lose money that way, but it is not long-term growth. Long-term value logically is determined by long-term growth of earnings and cash income per share. This must be based on a healthy, sustainable balance sheet, otherwise, it cannot be relied on.

Income per share is not a simple statistic either. Net income per share of a highly indebted or "leveraged" balance sheet is not as convincing a yardstick as net income of a company that has little debt. High interest charges will amplify the earnings range between a good and a not-so-good year, compared with a company that pays no interest. Thus the latter has greater earnings stability and is more apt to pay a dividend to the shareholders. Rising dividends based on rising net and cash income is one of my most desired indicators for investment. Earnings can be under- or overstated by all kinds of tricks.

These days you see frequent "special charges" or "restructuring." This normally leads to lower depreciation as major assets may have been written off. In turn, that overstates net income, though true cash income is relatively unchanged. This practice is not conservative, as depreciation should be defined as "wear and tear" plus "obsolescence," while the special charges reduce or eliminate obsolescence. If inadequate provisions are made for inventory or receivables, or if depreciation is insufficient, then there's a good chance again that net income is being overstated.

The **income tax rate** paid by a company is another important indicator to be considered. If you determine that it is too low for whatever reason, you should re-adjust it to a higher rate to get a truer recurrent rate. Then add back the cash savings (unless only deferred) as a bonus to be added to your valuation based on a normal multiple of earnings and cash income. That way you will not multiply a non-recurrent bonus as part of long-term valuation. Similarly, omit any other non-recurrent items contained in net income when determining what the "real earnings" are. A strict accounting exercise may come out slightly differently, but using these "rules of thumb" will bring you close enough.

These adjustments improve your analysis of the quality of earnings. If your earnings figures differ materially in either direction from the official figure given by the company, pose the question, "Why do they over- or understate earnings?" The answer will tell you a lot about management. If the earnings are overstated, you know that you have promotional management. You can cross-check this with bonus and option programs for top executives. If these are rich, you will realize that once the party is over, you may be in for a great fall – and sometimes Humpty Dumpty-like: "All the king's horses and all the king's men couldn't put Humpty together again!" If earnings are understated materially, there normally is also a reason: For instance, the company wants a low stock price. Usually in that case there is a controlling shareholder who cannot be dislodged by the small shareholders. He likes to buy shares cheap or he is worried about something else, such as estate tax.

Then there are "managed earnings." General Electric and many other stocks are cases in point. In good years, understatement is used and this is reversed in the poor ones, giving for many years an artificially stable pattern of growth. However, once no more "rabbits can be pulled out of the hat," you have to look reality in the face. So, as a rule, if you suspect managed earnings, be careful — and, again, watch the income tax rate. While I prefer that a company post real growth supported by its profits (provided, of course, that these haven't been manipulated), I am not opposed to them being very conservative in accounting of balance sheet risk. This stabilizes values and reduces greed and fear on the part of investors.

Net working capital is another item I watch. The current ratio, defined as current assets divided by current liabilities, is important in many companies. Current assets normally encompass largely cash, accounts receivable, and inventory, plus some prepaid items (taxes, rent, etc.). Current liabilities are made up of bank loans (short-term, i.e., under one year), trade payables, and some short-term accrued liabilities, plus long-term debt due within one year.

In the old days when I taught at university, we normally looked for a ratio of 2:1. In many industries, especially those that turn inventories over rapidly, this may be high today. Still, I want to know that all debts can be paid when they come due and that the company can take advantage of discounts on purchases by paying within 10 or 30 days, as the case may be. A deteriorating ratio worries me, as does a reduction of inventory turnover or a lengthening of the average receivable days outstanding. Good management will have enough foresight to control all these things to avoid jeopardizing "liquidity."

A strong balance sheet is something alert management can use for expansion or new opportunities, while a cramped one means constant struggle and opportunities that must be allowed to slide by. If a company's balance sheet is a few years ahead of itself I view that as a sign of strength, unless, of course, this causes management to rest on its laurels, which then is a sign of weakness.

Here, as in most things in life, the mean is opposed to both extremes. A company should neither be so adventurous as to risk everything and "bet the farm," nor play it so safe as to atrophy. Remaining balanced — always dynamic with its wits and brains fully alive — is what I look for.

Many balance sheets have an item on the asset side called "goodwill," especially companies that have made acquisitions paying above book value. Usually I place no value on the goodwill when I look at debt-to-equity or other ratios. It may or may not be worth something, but few companies write up their own fixed assets in their statements, so why place a value on it in an acquisition?

To ascertain good cost control, I look to ratios of different cost items to sales. Gross margin, sales expense, advertising, administration expense, etc., are meaningful in this regard. Also of interest are the ratio of net-income/gross-sales, and cash-income/gross-sales (cash income being net income plus amortization). If there are direct competitors, an inter-company comparison is informative. Good cost control indicates good management and, as we know, "a penny saved is a penny earned."

A good executive will strictly control his costs at all times and build a culture of economy that people take pride in. Profit margins should increase with volume, and if they do not, either poor cost control or sloppy sales effort — accepting losses on sales — is the reason. So if you see rising sales and stagnant profit, you should satisfy yourself that it is not due to poor management. Sometimes it is not. But then a sound long-term investment should only be in the low-cost producers with the best margins. The others may still grow, but the best will grow faster and keep paying dividends.

Many people look at **book value** and **return on equity**. I do look at them, but I have come to believe that they often don't mean much. A company that buys its own shares can bring book value to nil and still make lots of money. A company with a pile of goodwill has a high book value but less net tangible value. In a dying industry (steel, textiles), book value can be enormous, but no one builds new plants nor would it make sense to buy these assets at these prices. So book value sometimes reflects fair economic value, but not often. In regulated utilities this once had meaning, but as they are mainly deregulated now, it is no longer particularly useful.

All these balance sheet and income statement items, however, relate to the past. And the future, of course, is unknown. There are very few companies, in fact, where you can see further ahead than six months, if even that. There are just too many factors at play: company-related factors, industry-specific ones, and beyond that regional, national, and international factors.

Few, if any, of these factors remain stable. Airlines are possibly among the least stable companies, and because of this, as an investor I shun them at any price. Beer brewers, especially the leading ones, have the longest history of gradual stable growth, with only modest year-to-year variations due to fashion and weather. High-tech, apart from a semi-monopoly like Microsoft, is possibly the least predictable sector; the only thing you can predict in this sector is trouble. A competitor launching a new product first can destroy a company, while a discovery of their own will lead to a frantic burst of expansion. But such expansion will very likely be short-lived, as other competitors with a low entry threshold can be counted on to murder any good profit margin by coming out with the same product at a lower price. That's why I am not normally a high-tech investor.

I distinguish between industries for investment and industries for gambling. And not being a gambler, I concentrate my efforts on finding solid, stable companies. However, even these are not a completely safe bet these days. Communications worldwide have made for far more intense competition than before and regulation of industries has almost disappeared. Product standards are far stricter and lawyers, along with whistle blowers within companies, have made most businesses a veritable obstacle course. Add to this trade restrictions (despite free trade treaties), daily currency changes, minimum wages, and structurally inflexible employment practices, and you have a very difficult investment scene. If you want to avoid surprises, you should complement analysis, no matter how rigorous, with diversification.

Although security analysis along the traditional Graham & Dodd lines is absolutely essential, it deals only with past figures and doesn't provide anything more than guesses for the medium- and long-term future. Although companies now provide "guidance" on their expected future profit, these figures, as I know from operating businesses myself, are really nothing more than guesses. They can be based on budgets that are either optimistic or pessimistic and are susceptible to manipulation — and that, in any case, rarely come to pass. I never ask a company to predict earnings. That is my job as an analyst.

The key to the future does, however, lie partly in these figures of past years. History is a teacher and to not heed it is fraught with danger. The most valuable aspect of these figures, as I already hinted, is that they allow you to get some reading on the quality of management. I said before that management should be neither too adventurous nor too cautious. And a good balance sheet provides many clues about this. If the balance sheet is over-indebted, it indicates gamblers or past gamblers. Conversely, if it is too solid — swimming in cash with no debt — it points to a lack of imagination or ambition on the part of management. Further, excessive inventories point to a lack of discipline and inadequate cost control. Assessing management quality, therefore, is yet another vital component of sound security analysis.

Chapter 12

Factoring in Leadership

The true key to success is sound leadership coupled with a first-rate workforce — and a strong sense of teamwork uniting the whole. This is not to say that a focused and dedicated entrepreneur cannot single-handedly carry a company to great heights. But rarely does such a person have succession. Staff in such companies do not initiate things themselves, being accustomed instead to waiting for their leader's instructions. Once that leader is gone, the whole structure collapses and a total culture change becomes necessary.

We have seen that sleepy, poor, or even average management can today destroy not just smaller but also very large companies. AT&T, General Motors, IBM and U.S. Steel are only a few of the many examples. The world has become too competitive for anything but superb management — people devoted almost seven days a week and willing to commit long hours to the task. Prima donnas usually fail, as Enron, WorldCom, Tyco, and Vivendi have proven. Companies today cannot readily tolerate internal politics. Teamwork by very bright people is the key: People have to be able to work together harmoniously, knowing they can count on each other at all times.

Good management means not tolerating mediocrity and always trying to upgrade your staff. It means hiring quality young people and giving them responsibilities early to help them to develop leadership skills. It also means a good generational mix and a strongly defined culture that perpetuates itself. It means people who are willing to devote their lives to a company and fully accept their responsibilities at all times.

This asset, or lack thereof, is not stated on a company's balance sheet. As a matter of fact, you won't find it in the financial statements at all. Yet it is the most valuable asset the company has. Any securities analyst who does not concentrate on this asset misses the point of the exercise. Unfortunately, the majority of analysts fail the test.

To assume that all companies have good management and that all you need to do is look at ratios and cash income plus an assumed growth factor is to fall into an obvious error. A top analyst looks well beyond such figures — though you wouldn't know it from reading the newspapers or broker reports. It seems that with a CFA (Chartered Financial Analyst) designation practically anyone can be a "ratio analyst." I know but very few, however, who see the picture as I like to see it.

To thoroughly know an industry and the companies in it, an analyst must know about each company's lead director, whose job it is by law to "manage the company." That is, to know if a company is sound, you must know that the company's executive is first-class and will stay that way. As one old Swiss bank director once told me: "The most important thing in a business is to have had good management, as it sets the culture of the firm." Today it is necessary not just to have good management but to have superb management — and it is only superb if it is also providing for superb future management! I believe, in fact, that a corporate board's primary function is to assure the best management team.

It follows that an analyst should have a firm handle on the CEO's job. Unfortunately, most analysts sit alone in an ivory tower doing their ratios and reading all they can find on the Internet and in "investment studies." Hardly work that has them rubbing shoulders with people all day.

Although, of course, not all CEOs are alike, the really good ones have much in common. There are two principal types — the "hands-on executive" and the "delegator." Both know how to deal with people, with the second type being possibly better at that aspect of the job, while lacking the very important hands-on aspect.

Hands-on CEOs are typically more feared, as they tend to be perfectionists. They know the work and issues intimately and therefore can rely on their own judgment far more than delegators do. They live the company all day and all night, often seven days a week. A hands-on type CEO needs a very understanding spouse! These kinds of executives do not have to guess about people because they know exactly what it takes. They delegate to people who intimately share their vision and know that they must perform at top level at all times. The people who work with this kind of CEO are tuned in to their leader's philosophy and approach — to the point of being mind readers! — and only ask for help when they feel that something is not clear.

The delegator similarly has charisma; people like to work for delegators and strive to live up to the responsibility they have been entrusted with. Delegation-style CEOs have a more difficult choice of top people to trust, because they don't fully have that hands-on experience themselves and so must choose lieutenants who do. It may be argued that the delegator is the only type that can really head a large and intricate corporation, which requires multiple hands-on skills. Rare indeed are the executives who genuinely have such skills in all the main areas of a business. At Jarislowsky Fraser we are lucky to have two such people at the present time. If a company finds itself in this fortunate position and there is a good age difference, that may assure succession. But for this approach to keep working, the junior man must bring a yet younger man along fairly early in the game.

If what is actually the most valuable company asset — people — is stated at "nil" on the balance sheet, a security analyst must look beyond the figures. If you are a skilled analyst you will, in fact, concentrate most of your analysis on this factor. Why? Because good management is the only valid indicator that allows you to predict the future of a company. If the company has a sound culture and great people, these people will know what to do when circumstances change and will continue to do it well. They will work for the long-term success of the company and will express that commitment with all of their actions. They will not cut corners; they will read the signs of the future capably and adapt to them in short order. They will acknowledge errors and correct them and they will make sure that all the company's activities are staffed by the finest people. They will avoid senseless mergers and other ego trips. They will not take excessive risks and will make sure that slovenliness does not create unhappy surprises down the line. So if management is the key to all of this, analysts must be able to master this aspect of their research.

Actually, it is not that complicated. But what it takes is face-to-face knowledge of the people in an industry, and especially those in the best managed companies. You have to go out and meet them at regular intervals and talk to them. You also have to meet the competitors and find out which companies are the most respected and why. Once you have this information, you must update it regularly as things change daily. You must fully understand the culture of each organization because this so-called "intangible" really is a meaningful factor in an industry.

A key thing to understand is that good leadership takes character and the will to do what is right. Companies that gear their operations solely towards raising their stock values are suspect. The short term must be a reflection of the success of long-term values and strategies, not vice versa. This best serves the shareholder in the long run.

A good analyst should probably have served on a couple of boards to be able to see the inside of a corporation and observe management in action. Needless to say, it would also help if he had worked for a good sized company at some point, giving him the chance to observe how good or bad management functions and its impact on employees and on the workings of the whole company.

Having served on many boards over a 40-year period, I am quite familiar with the pitfalls of directorship. It takes a good board to assure good management in a public company. But if there is a majority shareholder who is more concerned with his own agenda than that of the rest of the shareholders, the task becomes near impossible. All a good director can then do is mitigate certain decisions. As an analyst, by and large I would avoid recommending the kind of company where ego plays a greater role than good practice and common sense.

I know analysts who visit companies but essentially talk only to the investor relations officer. This is not satisfactory. Investor relations officers are pretty unlikely to risk their jobs by providing anything more than the party line, certainly not unless they know you extremely well and know that you could keep any information that would endanger their job to yourself alone.

Similarly, speaking only to the CEO may not prove wholly satisfactory. The hands-on type of executive is usually concerned with immediate problems more than with a panoramic view, while the delegator often does not have specific facts of interest in his or her head. But it is important to get to know CEOs — especially the outstanding ones — as you can trust their judgment both about their own organizations and those of competitors. In the course of my career, CEOs often became my good friends, and some remain so to this day, though most are now retired. Their wealth of knowledge and informed viewpoints are invaluable in gathering information about the industry.

A good chief financial officer can also be very helpful — especially, again, if this person trusts you and your visit holds out the possibility of a two-way enrichment. I have frequently dug even deeper into organizations and asked the CEO if other top decision makers could sit in on our discussions. The very best field visits occur when a CEO invites one of her or his own associates to listen to your questions. This shows they recognize that you know the industry, their company, and the competition. This exchange of information becomes a two-way street, which can pay off enormously for you in the future. You become a "friend" of the company in their eyes. You will also find management much more forthcoming if you do not publish, and often this allows you to avoid mistakes that your information sources might not be able to forgive.

But your quest to ascertain good management does lead you back again to the figures, since competence or lack thereof can be followed quarter by quarter this way. Your field trip research provides you with certain expectations of a company's performance, and these expectations are either met or not as demonstrated in the quarterly statements. If not, you will want to get an explanation. A good management will admit mistakes. A poor one will attempt to disguise or rationalize them.

So how do you conduct an interview with management? How do you win management's confidence and esteem? Certainly not by blurting out, "How much per share do you expect to earn this year?" or, "Will you raise the dividend?"

Since CEOs regularly report to the board of directors, analysts should think about and ask the same kinds of questions as would conscientious board members. Analysts will also pose the same kinds of questions that CEOs ask of the employees who report to them. While good news is always easy to live with, serious CEOs always want to be fully informed about problems and potential problems above all, since these are the issues that require solutions and strategy.

When CEOs report to the board, they must know what kinds of questions their directors are likely to ask and have the answers ready, rather than having to say, "I will look into it." The CFO, who normally attends the meeting as a guest or resource person, must be even better informed than the CEO on any specific detail of the company's operations, apart from technical ones. So when an analyst asks questions that the CEO is normally asked internally, this is a process the executive is very familiar with, and the answers should be readily forthcoming. This is the test of a good executive: to be fully informed about the company's past and present with a definite, though changing, reckoning of the future.

For a high-level executive, the return on capital of the assets he supervises is very important. Also meaningful are leading products, product development, good margins, and controlled expense. These are the same issues that concern the board of directors. My approach as an analyst has typically followed a source and application statement analysis for the next year and longer. Cash income, financing, changes in net working capital (current assets minus current liabilities), capital expenditures, debt repayment, and last dividends are the major items I need information about.

Since I estimate net income myself, I ask for depreciation changes and financing intentions. Stock turns (inventory turnover), accounts receivable days outstanding, payment discounts, cash, and debt repayment needs — as well as the need for working capital — are some of the items I examine closely.

Capital expenditures and project completion dates for the next year, along with longer term suggested growth of sales and earnings, are also worth consideration. I then go over the sales figures with a fine-tooth comb looking at growth as well as any regression areas, and analyze the return on capital for each major division. This method allows me to spot management shortfalls or places where improvement is needed.

I am always leery of mergers and acquisitions, as they tend to change the corporate culture dramatically — for better or worse — and enormous management depth is required to carry them off successfully. I have learned that unless a company can put together a top team to integrate an acquisition, it should not normally venture out — unless the purchase has been made with the specific goal of acquiring a strong management team. As well, after the acquisition, it is key to put together a new team from both companies.

The last questions I ask as an analyst deal with the quality of the people, teamwork, and the cultural values of a firm. Normally, by this time I have gained the respect of the CEO, CFO, or whatever other executives I have been dealing with, because my questions have made them think and helped them to develop ideas of their own. The purpose of my interview is neither to get inside information nor to formulate precise forecasts. At this stage, I am simply completing my overall picture of the company, since I have already succeeded in evaluating what I believe to be the most important aspects: the company's place in its industry; its ability, based on management, to be among the very best as well as a low-cost producer in that setting; and its ability to improve its position. You eventually develop a "feel" for this!

Once you know the real decision makers in a company well and they respect you, you don't have to visit as often. Quarterly reports then generally give you all the information you need to assess whether the company is still on track. And, if they contain something surprising or raise questions, you can simply phone your contacts and get the answers.

The value of having good access to knowledgeable people cannot be over-estimated. It is essential to get a correct fix on an industry and the companies in it. If you leave too many "stones unturned" you may in time be in for some nasty surprises. It is important to remember that management's goal when talking to an analyst is to put a positive spin on a company. It is the analyst's job to probe the negatives and, in time, to arrive at a well-balanced impression. When putting the whole picture together, you should never underestimate the negatives, since it is those factors that can lead to real permanent losses, well beyond the superficial and temporary perceptions of the market.

Chapter 13

Looking for Warning Signs

There are many guideposts that can alert you to become skeptical about a company and the quality of its management. One I have already mentioned is **mergers**. Most mergers end in failure, even if they initially provide a few more cents of earnings per share. A retailer who vertically integrates normally lacks the skills of a manufacturing enterprise and vice versa. And cross-cultural restructuring is equally risky. A German company acquiring a competitor in North America, for instance, often does not know how North American companies are managed, nor does a German executive have the specific familiarity with the culture — corporate and otherwise — needed to lead a Midwestern company. And a foreign company that has recently acquired an American company may look in vain to hire an American to lead their new acquisition; in a country like the US all the well-qualified people have jobs already!

Consider the case of a small entrepreneur-led company that is bought by a larger company in the same sector. The seller will in all likelihood pocket the money without having any intention of continuing to work in the heart of the new enterprise; entrepreneurs rarely are compatible with large bureaucracies.

And some of the departed leader's best people will doubtless leave as well, especially if someone they do not respect or understand is placed over them. Morale is likely to plummet. At best, you will have two cultures in your company side by side. The list of problems is endless.

Then there is the problem of the entrepreneur who has built a large company. Once the company reaches a certain size, its creator can no longer have hands-on control over everything and, of course has no experience with delegating. Because the rest of the staff are not used to doing anything without their leader's specific instructions, once this person is gone the company is paralyzed. So after the entrepreneur's departure, everything needs to be reorganized from the bottom up and people need to be replaced or completely retrained. The result is often another failed company, especially if there is no succession of leadership. Similarly, when a son or daughter takes over a company built by their parent, they often try to continue to play the exact same role in the company their parent did — but frequently are unable to step into such large shoes. Corporate graveyards are filled with such examples.

If the company is a so-called "industry consolidator," the cultural problems again arise — unless the leader of the new entity is both a good financier and a leader who ruthlessly culls out all but the most valuable people from the consolidated companies. The attitude has to be "Take no prisoners!" If a consolidated company keeps only the best people who, in turn, have the skills to attract and motivate the best below them, it can end up with a successful hybrid culture. Sometimes this may work. But if the acquisitions are strictly based on companies with low price/earnings ratios being bought up to benefit the purchasing company, the new organization will eventually collapse, because it will end up with little leadership or incentive. A company run by someone who understands only financial engineering is on the road to disaster.

It is by no means guaranteed that a company that is debt free is also free of danger. Its debt load may suddenly soar if someone decides to use it as a vehicle for rapid expansion. High debt means higher costs, and trying to survive in a extremely competitive industry with high costs is always a precarious undertaking. Your risk in that case will suddenly have become much higher.

A caveat for field visits: Do not fall in love with a company or an industry. You may meet executives who try to charm and befriend you. This can be dangerous. You may end up letting your guard down and seeing things in a more rosy and less skeptical manner than you should. Never relax your vigilance and never stop questioning. A company that has done well in the market always looks better than one that has not. Their people may simply have a better flair for presentation. The less flamboyant company may, however, be the sounder.

Investment analysis is not cut and dried. It is always an art and develops with experience. The art consists in being able to form a gut reaction in response to all the research you have done, both technical and by interview. It is like art collecting in a way: A trained eye can immediately determine quality and take in the total picture. You develop an instinctive reaction. You tend to shy away from certain industries or companies, especially if your research doesn't give an integrated picture. Your gut is telling you there could be something wrong. Normally, it pays not to draw immediate conclusions but to watch a company for a year or more to make sure that you have not missed anything important.

This is especially true for fashionable industries or stocks. It is generally not a good idea to buy these, since fashions change and once the "hype" is gone, there will be many sellers for a long while. The high-tech sector for me is typical of this. No industry is more difficult to manage, since a company can fall off a cliff the moment someone else has a better mousetrap. And there is a mousetrap a minute out there! Entry is too easy, leading to almost constant and immediate over-capacity. Even the best companies typically only have a short life, and it is almost impossible to predict which will be among the few to succeed in the long term.

Mining and metal stocks, which are highly cyclical, are equally difficult to forecast and generally have lower long-term growth than the overall economy. In deep down cycles, the mines with heavy operating costs may be forced to close down, even though in periods of rising prices, their earnings accelerate the most. Buy this kind of stock only to take advantage of cyclical swings and only if the company's cost structure assures survival. Then be sure to sell at the right time, otherwise you may have to wait five years for another upward cycle. Airline stocks are best avoided entirely; in this industry, companies may stay alive at best. There is really no point in investing in recessive industries — it is far easier to swim with the stream than against it.

Try to focus on companies that will be around for a long time and that don't carry much danger of nasty surprises. Well-managed health care companies have served investors well in the past, though recently new conventional pharmaceutical discoveries have been much harder to come by. Chemical compound testing has diminished the chances of future major discoveries, as most substances have already been evaluated with new increasingly fast computer techniquee. Genome developments are a new frontier, but discoveries in this area tend to be applicable to specific groups of patients rather than to the entire human population at large. The group of drugs known as inhibitors looks promising, but side effects must be strictly controlled, because the litigation risk is enormous for all drugs that are not "seamless" (that is, they have minimal side effects). Tobacco and beverages are notable long-term industries, though the former also suffers from major litigation risk. Drug and food retailing has also proven itself — but only if well managed.

In finance, superior management is again essential. Poor investment poli-cies are a danger, since insurance companies and banks have a herd instinct, and quite regularly go over the cliff in droves. Everything in investment is transitory and perceptions change frequently. This is partly what makes it an art. Part of the art is in avoiding obvious error. You may not be perfect, but it is a relative game. "If you think I'm stupid, you should see the other guy!" Discipline is essential. Unlike some pundits who want to double or quadru-ple their money in a short time, I prefer the turtle approach over the rabbit one.

If I can find companies with a 12% annual long-term yield to buy, I'm delighted. This is a "compound growth rate" game. Obviously, the higher the rate, the faster the double. However, I prefer a steady approach to a yo-yo tra-jectory. Both can work, but the pedestrian one gets you there fairly pre-dictably, while the other, more exciting route, can be taxing and emotionally devastating. So my approach is to look for large companies, not small ones. A large company that runs into trouble will often get a second chance with renewed management. A small one rarely will.

Once your research is done, the question becomes: "At what price am I willing to buy and at what level am I willing to sell?" Since your aim is high annual compounding, clearly the lower you buy in, all factors otherwise being equal, the more you will make. If you establish a fair value for the entire com-pany, you can calculate what you are willing to pay for your shares from there. If growth is high and reasonably predictable and management is exemplary, obviously you should be willing to pay more. If it is an uninteresting compa-ny, you should probably pass entirely. Remember that the stock should fall within the parameters of your disciplined long-term investment policy if you are going to buy it, however exciting it may otherwise be.

Chapter 14

The Jarislowsky Foundation: Giving Sensibly

The Bible says it is more blessed to give than to receive, and I agree. Andrew Carnegie said, "It is more difficult to give money away intelligently than it is to earn it in the first place." I fully endorse this as well. One caveat is not to give to people who do not need charity — only to those who require charity to stay alive. Charity is for the needy, not the greedy! To paraphrase the Jewish philosopher Maimonides, the greatest charity is to give a beggar not a fish but a fishing rod with which to fish. The idea is to help people get back on their feet, gain self-respect, and become valuable members of the community.

Charitable giving, truly done well, is difficult and requires a lot of work and supervision. Charitable giving should be effective. It should achieve measurable goals. It should be implemented by people with integrity, and it should be fully researched so you know that your gifts will not end up in the wrong pockets. You should not give sentimentally, but insist on regular reviews of stewardship throughout the process. I don't believe in giving blindly. I also like to know what my giving will achieve and need to be comfortable with the cost.

Unfortunately, many charities are very inefficient, in that far too large a percentage of the money they receive ends up paying for fundraisers or administration. Many, even if the above does not apply, achieve only marginal results. Part of the problem is that they are often run by people who are underpaid or are outright volunteers, resulting in management that is less than the best.

What is the efficiency ratio of assistance funds lent or given to much of Africa or South America? How effective is money given for cancer, poverty, etc.? Unless you have a way of supervising your gift, often the only good it does is to make you feel good! In spite of their best intentions, do-gooders may fall into the hands of charities that are poorly designed, inefficient, or even downright dishonest. We have all heard stories about such phony or ineffective charities. But even solid organizations can achieve little if the work is not carried out by the most competent people.

Still, if you manage to build a large fortune, since leaving it outright to your offspring is rarely a good decision, you are likely to consider giving part of it away. "A shroud has no pockets," as they say. And if you can't use the money, someone else probably can! It is better to give money away during your lifetime than risk it being squandered afterwards.

In the past many cultures saw charity as a religious duty, if not as a guaranteed "way to heaven," and it was expected that people give a tithe (usually 10% of their income), normally to the church. In the US, charitable foundations are well established. We all have heard of some of the famous ones such as the Rockefeller, Ford, and Gates Foundations, but major new ones are formed regularly. In Canada, especially in French Canada, the idea remains new, but is spreading rapidly. Very few foundations in Canada have over $100 million. The formation of community foundations, which amass whole estates, has begun to spread and many western Canadian cities have one.

But, as we have said, giving intelligently is hard work and supervising the gifts intelligently even harder. To do it well, you need to define a policy of giving and then stick to it. This is what we are attempting to achieve with the Jarislowsky Foundation, which was formed some 12 years ago to receive earnings not allocated to specific partners of our firm. While varying from year to year, this normally is equivalent to some 2 to 7% of our pre-partnership unallocated income, that is to say, income net of all cash costs other than the salaries and profit participation of the partners (but pre-tax of course).

The Jarislowsky Foundation has accumulated some $50 million in funds to date, which is held in a variety of investments based on our normal investment criteria. Our policy is to give away the equivalent of 4.5% of market value of this amount per annum, or some $2 million a year currently[2].

The foundation has a board of three people and no paid employees. My assistant and I do most of the work. Our main mission is "excellence," as opposed to the Canadian trait of mediocrity. Our work is largely confined to one area — university chairs in Canada. But we also give for excellence in a few other areas, including medical instruments and unusual medical research. We have supported as well a number of cultural causes, ranging from the Montreal International Literary Festival to the Canadian Opera Company and the Canadian War Museum.

But by far our largest annual outlay is for university chairs. We have now endowed 12 chairs in total, the latest being the 2004 chair at the University of Windsor in "Comparative Religion" and a chair in Conflict and Religion at the University of Windsor. These days we give $1 million for endowment of a new chair. So more than 50% of our giving is in this one annual gift. It is

---

[2]   Jarislowsky Fraser also has many charitable foundations as clients, including hospital and university endowment funds, for which it manages funds. Its investment management fees to these charitable funds are generally lower than for other funds, in acknowledgement of their missions.

this concentration of giving that makes our work relatively simple. If funds are left over at year-end, we try to further back one or two of our most successful chairs with supplementary gifts.

Our chairs are very financially efficient and have the added benefit of supporting superb teaching and research in areas we feel need to be addressed — for the very long term. We demand 100% matching by the university and often also by the wider public. Moreover, in many cases, we benefit from provincial or federal government matching programs. As a result, our chair at the University of Alberta started with 300% of our gift. This process, plus long-term growth of the invested funds above the 4.5% pay-out, results in these chairs becoming extremely well-endowed over time.

With each chair we aim for national, or better yet international, calibre in its area of teaching and research. It is enormously important to have the right chair holder. We consider teaching and charisma to be essential for attracting top students from around the world and for developing an influence that extends well beyond one's own university. Research, in addition to being or becoming renowned in one's area of expertise, is also a must. Let us not forget our own university experience! How many professors had a profound influence on us? How many do we honestly remember throughout our lives? It is this kind of role model we seek for the chair holder.

The discipline chosen has to be one that has and will continue to have thrust in building the university's reputation. At McGill University, it is medicine (urology). At the University of Montreal, international project management (engineering). At Concordia, fine arts (Canadian art). At the University of Saskatchewan, biotechnology. At the University of Guelph, families and work. At McMaster University, environment and health. At the University of Ottawa, public sector management.

The chairs are run typically by a committee of five people who review its activities: two from the university, two outsiders (normally in the discipline), and one member of our foundation. This way we avoid a good part of university politics. Chair holders normally have a five-year mandate once the right person has been found. Interim people may be nominated at start-up but only for a year or two.

Our university chair initiative has been very successful. With relatively modest funds, initially tax deductible, we have leveraged the investment of far larger sums and, since the money is for endowment, the funds have grown even more. These funds have a long-term future and should offset inflation and then some. The close supervision of the chair as well as the outstanding ability of the chair holders gives us some confidence that the funds are being well used.

The endowment status, which protects the foundation's capital and ensures that only the earnings from it are distributed, provides the flexibility to make changes if mistakes are made (such as the selection of a poor chair holder). For its part, the university can enhance its reputation and attract well-known names based on the ability to pay more and to give a prestigious appointment. On our side, we are able to keep our expenses to an absolute minimum (nil to date!), since the establishment of only one chair a year requires little administration. And often, as I have mentioned before, these chairs attract additional research money each year from government or industry.

This experience in charitable donation has been very effective in bringing excellence at relatively low cost to 12 different universities. Not only has this venture worked out well but it is giving my wife and me a great deal of pleasure. Looking ahead, I believe the foundation will continue to play a major role in developing Canadian university expertise for many, many years to come. At the same time, with its current rate of annual giving, the foundation will also be able to continue to accumulate substantial funds. And as a result at a certain point, it will be able to take on broader and more complicated missions.

Our foundation model could be emulated by others for many themes. You could, for instance, give to the poor in Africa and work to reduce the ravages of AIDS there. However, this would require working through agencies or government with the result that you would have far less ability to gauge the results. This is not something I feel I can do effectively. A friend of mine works principally on teaching entrepreneurship; yet another on nursing in hospitals. All are worthwhile initiatives. I am not, however, interested in giving to projects that I believe should be financed by our taxes — university buildings, new hospitals, etc.

Unfortunately, our governments have not shown themselves to be especially effective in providing funding for these much-needed services. On the other hand, they are very good at taking money out of our pockets and spending it unwisely. In some cases, the private sector has no choice but to step in and take the initiative. Along with partners such as Manulife Financial, we have done this in the area of prostate cancer awareness. For two years Manulife has underwritten a website based in Quebec that provides a wide variety of information about this disease, which is not well understood by the public. I believe raising awareness and promoting prevention could go a long way towards helping people detect prostate cancer early and ultimately improve their longevity and quality of life. This public education initiative is an effective approach that can bear enormous fruit and is in keeping with my philosophy of giving.

Chapter 15

Like What You See
in the Mirror

Intelligently managing your affairs over many years is a difficult challenge. It is especially tricky for the small investor with under $500 000. People with significantly less money to invest may not find individually tailored investment counsel worth the cost. Yet the small investor needs advice as much as a wealthy person in order to amass an ever-growing nest egg over the years. And quite often such small investors just get "ripped off" by those who profess to want to help.

The broker looks for maximum commissions; the financial planner looks to maximize his fees, either directly or through commissions from products recommended; banks are usually unimaginative; the mutual fund takes far too large a "load" at entry and exit and charges an excessive operating fee, etc. A lawyer and an accountant may also get into the act. The result is a lack of clear policy, lack of a clear objective, excessive attention to tax rather than investment, and so on. Time and money that should be compounding the investment are wasted.

Big employers have abdicated their investment responsibility for pension plans and have shifted it onto the employee through defined contribution plans. This means that, rather than a guaranteed pension at retirement, you in effect get your own fund (employee and company contribution) and can yourself, within limits, choose how to invest it: short-term money, bonds, common stocks, or a combination.

However, few people know what is good for them and so most tend to choose bonds (since stocks in a fearful mind are deemed risky). This, as you of course know after having read this book, is the wrong solution. Or they choose mutual funds (expensive again), which are not normally tailored to the highest compound growth rate at low risk. As a matter of fact, most mutual funds will underperform the main stock market indexes. Someone will explain your options and tell you what is suggested at certain age levels, but knowing little and being a bit cautious, you may opt for bonds or cash.

If you are still young — under 40, say — you will not be very concerned. Retirement is way down the road. So why worry about it? This is a cardinal mistake, as I have made clear. The time to let compound growth work for you is at birth or as soon thereafter as feasible. In 40 years, a double every five years may raise $10 000 to $2.5 million. Why not be a millionaire at 40?

The fact is that everyone under 60 years of age should essentially opt for common stocks of the type I propose. I assume retirement at age 65. Ten years before your retirement date you should take a close look at your asset mix (the division between my kind of stocks and short-term money). If you have a few million accumulated, remain essentially in stocks, unless markets are very high. If they are very high, as they are today, place half the funds in a staggered bond portfolio in which the average term to maturity is, say, 5 to 6 years.

If markets are average, stay largely in stocks, possibly transferring 10% of the portfolio every two years to short bonds, for a total of 50% at retirement. If your total retirement money is less than $1 million, you should accelerate this process if stocks are at average or high valuations, so as not to be caught with a bad market at retirement. However, even here I would not desert stocks entirely if less than five years are left before retirement. Even with fairly small sums, I would probably continue to keep 25% in stocks, especially in times when inflation is a factor. Stocks in time overcome inflation. Cash and bonds do not.

During all the years before retirement, and even right up until five years before (except in times of excessive market valuation), I would remain in stocks on the high compound growth highway. Remember that if you can double your money every five years, your last five years should provide as much as all the years before put together. In an average priced stock market, this is not a period to abort your program.

If your pension plan dictates that you must buy mutual funds, and you have a choice, look for those that espouse the policies of this book and have very low operating costs (1% maximum). The Dow Jones Industrial Average contains many stocks that fit my bill. If nothing better is available, buy a Dow Jones Industrial Average index fund. Chances are you will do well and the operating costs are minimal. Be sure also to have the maximum foreign content permitted by law, and in Canadian shares, go for a quality stock fund. Canada has few of the kind of growth stocks I have described. This is due to the fact that our economy remains very resource-oriented and to date we have developed very few non-cyclical, high-quality, international growth companies. Chances are that in the long term, Canadian stocks will underperform your foreign portfolio.

It may be wise to look at the stocks in the portfolio of your pension fund to see whether they fit the bill and will allow you to realize your retirement goals. If not, find out whether other funds are available that more nearly give you what you want. If something is good for you, it may well also work for your co-employees.

If you have an RRSP, have a self-directed one and at age 69 convert it to a Registered Retirement Income Fund. This will permit you to continue to invest your money cheaply and intelligently during your entire life.

Moreover, in your early years, try to maximize savings for a while in order to take advantage of the many years of compound growth. As you get to the other side of 40, make sure you don't only save but enjoy life as well. As you may well have a tidy nest egg by then, saving additional funds is not as essential, since the time horizon for compounding is shrinking in any case. This is the time to expand your material horizons — within your income and on a sustainable basis, of course.

I don't believe that a small investors should abdicate responsibility, believing that the task is beyond them. By learning to use some simple, well-tested yardsticks and acting on them in a disciplined manner, they should do very well. Go for long-term growth and top-quality and be a patient, long-term investor.

Some final advice, this time of a different sort. Use your life for the good. Remain loyal to your mentors, your colleagues, and especially your family and friends. It is the last two you need most when you get old. Even when fortune smiles, remain simple in your lifestyle, but without being niggardly. Look for real values in your life and practice them. Give everyone the benefit of the doubt. But strictly avoid the bad guys; act with and expect total integrity, and keep as distant from those who do not live up to this standard as you can. Above all, be sure that you like what you see in the mirror!